Soaring
on Broken
Wings

Soaring on Broken Wings

A Story of Triumph in Tragedy

by

Kathy Bartalsky

MOODY PRESS

CHICAGO

ISBN: 0-8024-2316-7

1 3 5 7 9 10 8 6 4 2

Printed in the United States of America

*Eternally dedicated to
my loving husband, Steve,
my charming son Colby,
my beautiful daughter, Christina,
and the continuing joy of my life,
Steven Louis*

Contents

Foreword

When a young woman determines in her heart to learn what "faith in God" means, and asks Him to teach her, what happens? God hears the prayer and begins to answer it—not in a lecture hall but right where that woman lives. She begins day by day to believe that the God of the universe is also the God of the fallen sparrow. He made sparrows. He loves sparrows. He also made and loves her, and she has His word for it that she is of more value than many sparrows. He will prove it to her, as He proved it to the whole world long ago, through the mystery of suffering.

Kathy Bartalsky is a woman consumed with hunger to know Him. Parachute jumping taught her a few principles of trust. Committing to God her very deep and womanly desire for a husband taught her more. God gave her a good and loving man, and they began together to learn the lessons that the answer to her prayer for faith entailed.

She tells her story straight. We are taken into the couple's anxieties about having children. It was a clear choice at that point: either they would trust God, or they would not trust Him. "It is always easier to trust Him," she writes.

But the lesson must be reviewed. Her husband failed to get a promotion. The agony of job-hunting went on and on. Money problems, housing problems, marital tensions provid-

9

ed what turned out to be merely the elementary lessons of the course in knowing God for which both had registered. New situations arose in which Kathy found herself "fighting to keep my direct influence rather than just see this as an opportunity to surrender my struggles and rely on the sovereignty of God's will." She tells us of her fears, her mistrust of God's plan for her life, of how hard it was and is to bring both heart and emotions to a place of peace. But gold, of course, must be refined. It takes very hot fires to burn dross. If it's gold you want, you take the fire.

Kathy wanted gold. She knew academically that there would be fire. This would be the advanced course, and it came. She and Steve went through it and learned more of who God was and what it meant to trust Him. The death of a child was not the end of the purifying process. When she thought, *Why do I get the feeling this isn't going to be easy?* God reminded her of His faithfulness to His promise: *You will come forth as gold. It's what you asked for, isn't it?*

Chapter after chapter revealed what I was tempted to feel was more than one woman could possibly bear. What did I know of flames? Most readers, I suppose, will feel the same. But keep reading—we need to look long and hard, from the perspective of our own lives, at God's unfailing tenderness and faithfulness in another's life. We find it in the Bible, of course, in every life story told there. But we need also to find it in the late twentieth century, in America of all places.

Kathy bore the fires as thousands in Christian history have borne them—by faith, by grace, by the blood of the Lamb. She was *committed* to Christ. Her surrender was never negotiable. It was His pathway she had chosen, a pathway that always leads to a cross. She accepted that cross, believing that *that* death leads always to the glory of resurrection.

It was hard for her to trust that, because of His love for her, He allowed such pain into her life to shape her heart. Yet she trusted, looking far past the seemingly unbearable temporal things to the eternal perspective. Hers is the "victory that overcomes the world"—that miracle of grace that learns that suffering is something *granted*, a blessing, or, as she says, "more appropriately an honor"—not meant for herself alone but, in identification with Christ and His cross, for the sake of the world.

"We accept as common knowledge that God can save a sinner, yet we do not wholeheartedly believe that God can and will sustain a believer."

Here is evidence beyond argument of that mighty sustenance.

ELISABETH ELLIOT

1
A New Life

I dove out the door and with increasing speed plunged toward the earth. I looked around for Harold and Perry and caught sight of them just above me, silhouetted against the small Cessna that was now flying back to the drop zone. My speed had picked up to about 120 miles per hour, and I settled into a stable "belly to earth" position as I waited for Harold or Perry to fly down to me. The excess length of my helmet strap, which I had tucked inside my helmet, worked its way out and with the force of the wind rhythmically began to whip against my face.

Perry came down in front of me about seven feet away and began to make a gentle approach toward me. In a few seconds we linked together, grasping hands firmly. Harold came in toward my left, grabbed our wrists, and nodded for the break. Perry and I dropped hands on Harold's side so that he could grab our hands. We looked at each other with big smiles. Harold nodded again, and as we had planned on the ground, Perry broke free and turned 180 degrees. Harold and I each quickly grabbed the leg nearest us.

Once we were securely locked in that position, I looked down at the altimeter on my belly strap and saw that we had about twelve seconds left before we needed to open our chutes. I nodded to Harold for the break. We let go of Perry, who immediately went into a dive leading away from us. I was just about to nod to Harold for our break when he pulled me in for a quick "kiss pass." I could never get away from those guys fast enough to avoid their little mid-air romances! I turned 180 degrees in order to put enough distance between Harold and me for a safe opening and went into a dive. When I pulled up out of the dive, I looked around to see Harold far to my left, Perry already under his chute, and a clear sky above me. I waved my hands to signal that I was about to open. Harold did the same, and together we pulled our little pilot chutes from their pouches, threw the chutes into the open air, and braced ourselves for the opening impact.

My main parachute stretched out of its container and opened with brisk force, pulling the harness even more snugly around me. I looked up to see that all the air cells of my new black and red square-shaped canopy were opened, so I could fall confidently to the ground. The slower rate of descent relieved me from the constant whipping of my loose helmet strap, and I comfortably absorbed the peacefulness around me.

Slowly I began to take in the panorama that hemmed me in on all sides. I always enjoyed the quiet beauty of the surroundings and the gentle flapping of my parachute in the breeze as I fell to the drop zone. I could see for miles and viewed the world from the perspective of a bird in lofty flight, carried by the up-currents of the winds. Although the earth below looked big and majestic, the life on it seemed small and insignificant, as if it were swallowed up by a larger meaning or purpose. I thought about God and His omniscience and constant presence in the affairs of man. *What is His greater purpose for this world? How can I—one person who seems destined for mediocrity—fit into that plan?*

It wasn't long before I had to focus suddenly on the immediate reality before me. The ground was coming up to me rapidly, rather than my softly descending, so I pulled on the right toggle line to set up for a downwind approach to the drop zone. About 250 feet from the ground I made another

14

right turn to glide onto the base side of the landing field. Once I was above the target area, I made a final right turn to face upwind and slow down my ground speed. The winds were calm, and I estimated that my forward speed was still racing at about thirty miles per hour. I adjusted the flare of my canopy carefully so that I wouldn't crash into the ground. Finally, not more than ten feet in the air, I pulled down hard on both toggle lines. That caused my canopy to "stall" or stop in flight for a few seconds, supposedly enabling me to step onto the ground as easily as walking down a flight of stairs, though my skills at "walking" out of the sky usually left me with a knee digging into the grass. I landed safely. It was another successful jump.

How I loved skydiving! And how my skydiving worried my mother. She couldn't understand why her only daughter loved to do something so completely insane. And although I was only twenty-one years old, she kept wondering when I was going to become a little more domestic. Why couldn't I be more interested in needlepoint or cooking? Or marriage? Actually, I did enjoy other hobbies and even entertained the idea of marriage, but I loved the sport of skydiving. I was thrilled by the excitement of free-falling and the adventure of landing into someone's unmarked cow pasture.

The first several jumps were frightening, but once I got past the first dozen or so without a major incident, I began to relax and enjoy my newfound skill. I got so involved in the sport I was awarded the "C" (advanced) license issued by the United States Parachute Association and was able to jump in a Blue Angels Air Show as part of the parachute demonstration team.

I was serving on active duty in the navy at the time, working as an oral surgeon's technician at a naval hospital on the Cherry Point Marine Corps Air Station in North Carolina. My military standing allowed me many privileges. One of the more memorable took place after I was elected vice-president of the Cherry Point Skydiving Club.

As a new member of the board, I participated in discussions regarding the possible use of helicopter support from the base helicopter squadron. If we could get permission to use a marine helicopter on base facilities, we would not have to make a two-hour drive every weekend to the civilian drop zone. The men on the board decided that, since I was the vice-president and the only female in the club, I should have the privilege of asking the helicopter squadron for its help. I would be all the more effective, the men thought, if the pilot I approached was single. This devious plot did not originate in the manipulative mind of a woman skilled in her art, but in the minds of grown *men*. They were plotting and scheming against the weakness of their own gender!

I got in touch with a friend named Joe Fryman, a crew chief for the helicopter squadron. As crew chief, Joe assisted the pilots in various functions during take-offs, landings, and search and rescue operations. He knew all the helicopter pilots, and when I told him of the board's "requirements," he suggested someone named Steve Bartalsky, one of only two single pilots, boasting that Steve was the best pilot the squadron had.

Steve agreed to meet with me, and we set up a meeting in a honky-tonk restaurant. To arm himself for the meeting, he brought three of his marine friends just in case he needed help in getting away from some macho military woman who jumped out of airplanes. He thought I would be built like a tank, look like a dog, and think like a true navy squid (the nickname for navy personnel because they are a "lower form of marine life").

I admit that my mental pictures of him were not very romantic either. Our meeting was to take place after he was finished bowling with his league. *Well*, I thought, *not only is he a marine jarhead, but the lid's on tight as well!*

But I got reasonably dressed up anyway and went hoping for the best. Joe came over to greet me when he saw me come in and then led me to the table. Steve was sitting with his friends in a booth near the back of the restaurant. He was noticeably surprised when he saw me and quickly rearranged everybody so that I would be directly across from him. I asked

16

him what the possibilities were of the jump club's using his squadron's helicopters but soon discovered that he did not have the authority to give us the permission we needed. Frustrated, I began to wonder why he had even agreed to meet with me. He must have known already that he wouldn't be able to answer my question. Joe must have known it, too. Suddenly I realized *I* was the one who had been set up, for by the end of the evening, Steve had asked me out for our first date.

It didn't surprise me when he picked me up a few nights later to find that we were headed to a movie called *The Great Santini*. To what other movie would a dedicated marine aviator take a first date? Nevertheless, it was a fun evening, and his easygoing manner made me feel relaxed. Before we parted, he made it clear that he wanted to see me again. But after that movie, I couldn't imagine what gung-ho event would be next.

It didn't take me long to find out. Steve asked me to the Marine Corps Officers' Ball—a little more elegant and romantic than *The Great Santini*. I wore a peach-colored gown from a wedding in which I had participated, and Steve, a little nervous and a little late, showed up at my apartment in a full dress white uniform, complete with ribbons and medals and looking extremely handsome. It was to be an enchanted evening.

I soon learned that Steve was not as boring as his bowling league image had projected. Once we were among his peers, his true colors began to show as he proudly paraded me before his superior officers and insisted that we be posed for permanent history in front of every camera lens in the place. The lid on that marine jarhead was definitely not screwed on all the way. I learned that Steve's peers knew him as "Shadow." His friends in college gave him that name because he slipped in and out of his room so quietly his movements couldn't be noticed. His roommates finally put a sign on their door that read, "The Shadow is:" and Steve would flip the

17

card to the appropriate answer—either "in" or "out"—so that they could keep track of him.

Steve was well-liked and had many close friends. He came from a large family, and because his father was a fighter pilot in the Air Force, he had grown up in many diverse cultures. Those cultures had shaped his ideas and broadened his perspective of his role in the world. They had taught him also to accept people for who they were. When he went to college the degree he earned was in international relations.

After completing college, he began a career in the military, intending to serve his country as a marine officer. He had inherited a love for flying from his father and wanted to follow in his father's footsteps as a jet pilot. But he was not assigned to fly jets. Instead, he was assigned to helicopter training—and he came to love it, flying low and slow, forgetting his desire to race across the sky. I saw a wonderful stability and gentleness in Steve's attitude toward people and toward life in general. He was a quiet person at first meeting, but he was loyal to his beliefs and his relationships were very strong.

At the age of twenty-eight Steve was seven years my senior, and my own immaturity and inexperience next to such quiet adaptability were evident. Nevertheless, we fell in love, and six months later Steve proposed to me. We actually had to make our decision rather quickly because we were each due to rotate for new duty stations in six months. Steve already had orders to go to Hawaii, and we both knew that I would probably be headed overseas to Spain or Italy for a short-term commitment before getting out of the navy in eighteen months.

Since Hawaii was considered a desirable duty location, we had to convince my detailer (the person who assigned my next location) that we were indeed serious about getting married and not trying to fabricate a reason for me to go to Hawaii. We found that in order for me to get orders to Pearl Harbor, I would have to extend my commitment to Uncle Sam for an additional nineteen months. That would make a total of three years of duty in Hawaii. It was not difficult at all to make the decision to extend my commitment. I wanted to be with Steve, and my job as an oral surgeon's technician was very much like the nine-to-five job I would have had in the civilian world. Working in Hawaii would definitely not be a sacrifice.

With the logistics behind us, we planned for the wedding. It was to be August 30, 1980—just three days after Steve's twenty-ninth birthday. Preparations and details flooded my days, while dreams of being a radiant bride filled my mind at night. They were happy days, for even my father was pleased with my choice of a husband-to-be. Steve was the first and only man ever to receive my father's approval. My father saw in Steve a soft-spoken yet secure person. He recognized Steve's maturity. Steve never needed to defend or to prove himself. It was easy to recognize Steve's sincerity with people and his willingness to serve. The fact that he held the impressive rank of captain in the Marine Corps only pushed him over the top in my father's eyes.

We were to be married at Olivet Presbyterian Church in Harrisburg, Pennsylvania, the church in which I had grown up. There as a little girl I had learned the stories of Jesus and there at the age of twelve had made public confession that I wanted to know Jesus as my personal Savior. I don't really remember a time when I didn't understand that Jesus was Lord and that He had died for my sins, though for several years when I was a teenager I had tried to ignore God, experimenting with drugs, alcohol, and sex, and moving out on my own at the age of seventeen. Yet as I matured, I was drawn back to the truth that had taken root in my heart when I was a small child. The closer I came to my wedding day, the more serious I became about recommitting my life to Christ.

Steve, too, was feeling a definite tug in his heart as our wedding day approached, and we talked about the faiths of our childhood. Steve had grown up in a large Catholic family and had never forgotten that he was supposed to know, love, and serve God with all his heart. I knew that marrying outside the Catholic church was a difficult choice for Steve, but he had often said, "My deeper desire to love Jesus and understand His love for me make a far greater impression on me than my fears about being cast from heaven simply because I marry a Protestant." We decided to let God teach us and bring us into a harmony of worship that would best glorify Him. So on our wedding day, as we spoke our vows publicly to God and to each other, we began a fresh new life together with Jesus.

The wedding was beautiful, but I remember thinking that considering the amount of anxiety we had experienced as we made preparations, it should have lasted longer than twenty minutes. We came out of the church through a small military sword arch, kissed, and dreamed of living happily ever after.

2
Steven Louis

Two months later we packed up our belongings and left our North Carolina beach house in the hands of a local realtor to lease out. We were on our way to the island of Oahu in the tropical paradise of Hawaii.

The first part of our journey was by car, and the trip across the country was, in part, our honeymoon. We stopped to see family and friends along the way, but the most enjoyable times were spent driving through the night hours, just talking. One evening as we crossed the deserts of Arizona and during my turn at the wheel, Steve pulled out an old, thin book. He turned on the vanity light on his sun visor, leaned back against the door, propped up his feet in my lap, and began to read me *The Old Man and the Sea*. For the next hour, we were no longer surrounded by cacti and dry heat but were struggling with an old man in a shabby boat on a distant sea, cold and soaked to the bone, desperately clinging to a dream.

Just a week later we flew over the beautiful, warm, blue seas around the Hawaiian islands, and our dream became a reality. But it didn't take us long to learn that though we were stationed on the same island, we worked worlds apart. Steve's marine base was located on one side of the island, and the Pearl Harbor Dental Facility where I was to work was on the other. We finally decided to live on his side of the island because it was less traveled by the tourists. The islanders called it the "windward" side because constant gentle tradewinds blessed its sandy shores. The choice meant that I had to drive each day over the "Likelike" (pronounced "leaky-leaky") highway to the "leeward" side (meaning "sheltered"), where I worked as the head technician in the oral surgery department.

It took us a month to find a home that met our needs, but we finally bought a condominium on the Kanoehe Bay. Our dream was becoming everyday life. We began to make friends, and I met many of the other pilots' wives whose husbands were in the same squadron as Steve. These friendships deepened rapidly in the four months before we stood on the docks of the Pearl Harbor shipyard and said farewell to our husbands. For six months the men would be deployed with the naval ship *Bellowwood* on the Indian Ocean, practicing military maneuvers and "showing the flag."

While he was gone, I decided to undergo diagnostic surgery for a medical problem that had long bothered me. I had always suffered from severe cramping and bleeding, and surgery the year before had indicated that I had large adhesions and scarring throughout my reproductive organs, but that particular surgery had not been conclusive. So in March I admitted myself to Tripler Medical Center, a large army research facility. After the surgery, the doctor confirmed the presence of the adhesions and scarring. He told me that he had removed some of the larger adhesions but that there were still quite a few left. That was bad enough, but he said as well that there was extensive scarring throughout the inner walls of my fallopian tubes. I probably would not be able to conceive children without micro-surgery to remove that scar tissue.

Before I left his office, the doctor told me that my chances of conceiving would be best within a year of the recommended tubal surgery; even then, my chances for conceiving would be four in ten, and a tubal pregnancy would still be possible. The figures were far from encouraging, but he did say that because he had removed the large adhesions, my cramping might be less painful. That was as about as comforting as he could be.

Needless to say, the news was disappointing. I so wanted to have children. Shortly after that, I learned that Steve was flying home from the Philippines, where his ship was docked, so that he could be with me. Although I hadn't wanted to worry him about the surgery, I was happy to find that he was coming home. I shared the diagnosis with him and repeated the figures the doctor had given me. When we were in North Carolina Steve had known that I was having problems and that the threat of not being able to have children was real. He had told me then, and now he reconfirmed, that having children and raising a family wasn't an important issue for him. He loved me for who I was. If we decided to have the surgery, it would be because we had prayed and knew that the Lord was directing it. Steve was very comforting. Nothing seemed to ruffle him, and he brought to the surface what I already knew in my heart to be true—that if the Lord wanted us to have children, it didn't matter what the doctors said. I was content with the knowledge that my menstrual pain would be decreasing.

Steve had to go back to the Philippines before his ship left port, so a few days later we said good-bye again and continued our love through the mail. As hard as it was to be apart, I wouldn't trade the letters he wrote to me for anything. Like most men, he was not flowery or overly romantic in what he said in person, but in his letters he clearly articulated the feelings of his heart for me. One such letter came shortly after his return to the Philippines:

Dearly Beloved Wife,

How are you doing? I would think that you are very well because of my prayers for you, and my total love and devotion. If you could just feel a fraction of all the emotions I have for you, you would be feeling good for a long, long time. I want you to know that I love you more today than yesterday, and I am positive that tomorrow I'll love you even more! I'll bet you've heard that before, but Kathy, I mean every word from the bottom of my heart! I do realize that you are a jewel amongst trinkets, a rose amongst daisies . . . and I am miserable sitting over here in the middle of the Indian Ocean away from you physically and spiritually.

I eagerly look forward to tomorrow because I'll have some letters from you when we reach the next port. I'm so excited!

I love you, Babe. Miss you. Take care. Drink milk. God bless you.

Forever in love (with you),
Steve

His first deployment went by without incident. Toward the end of it my parents came to visit. They arrived in the first part of July, and I was overjoyed that they were able to be with me on July 28, one day after my twenty-third birthday, the day Steve was coming home. We were filled with excitement and anticipation as we watched the squadron of helicopters fly over the Hawaiian mountains toward the hangar building where all the wives anxiously waited to meet their husbands. Military homecomings are emotionally high-powered, whether one is there as a wife or as an observer.

Steve had only been home a month when I noticed that I had missed a month of my regular "pain sessions." I didn't think much about it because I was irregular anyway. But after six weeks went by, we decided to do a pregnancy test. It came back negative, and although I really believed that the problem was related to my gynecological problems, I was disappointed.

The doctor told me that even though the test results were negative, I could be hosting a tubal pregnancy, which is more difficult to diagnose than a normal pregnancy; so I should be prepared to come in at the first sign of pain. That warning was particularly disturbing—every day I expected massive pain to tear through my body, and I envisioned myself being wheeled into the nearest emergency room.

A few more weeks went by with little change in my condition. Steve insisted that I take another pregnancy test. I

24

didn't want to face the possibility of another negative answer, but I had the test done one morning and tried to keep as busy as possible at my job. The young hospital corpsman said I could call sometime after 2:00 that afternoon to get the results. The intervening hours seemed an eternity.

At 2:01 everyone I worked with gathered around the phone as I dialed. I gave my name and listened. When I hung up the phone, my co-workers still could not tell what the results were. There was a numb look of shock on my face. I was pregnant.

I set up an appointment with the doctor and discovered that I was about twelve weeks along. He could already hear the heartbeat, but he cautioned me to be careful because of my physical history. In mischievous pleasure I had to say, "I thought you said this couldn't happen!" He replied, "Oh, what do doctors know?" I thought, *How right you are. God alone knows.*

And it was not just that this pregnancy was a surprise to the doctors. Steve and I were impressed as well by the fact that the Lord had answered our prayer long before we had ever presented it to Him as a serious request. We knew precious Scripture verses concerning God's faithfulness—"He settles the barren woman in her home as a happy mother of children" (Psalm 113:9); "but you, O Lord, are a compassionate and gracious God, slow to anger, abounding in love and faithfulness" (Psalm 86:15)—but we had not let worries over whether we would have a family consume us. I believe that God honored our simple faith in Him. In just a few short years, my life was to change dramatically, and I was to learn how important this principle of choosing to trust God was. In each situation I was to face I always had the choice of trusting or not trusting God. It was always easier to trust Him.

Although the pregnancy went along beautifully, the doctor treated it as a complicated pregnancy. Steve was due to go out to sea again before the delivery, but we sought special permission from his superiors all the way up to the general of the base, and finally he was allowed to stay home for the birth.

Late one afternoon, during the fourth month of my pregnancy, Steve and I were out walking and enjoying the cool breezes by the bay. As we watched the sailboats slowly change the seascape and leisurely float over the surface of the rich blue water, we began to discuss the possibility of my quitting the navy to become a full-time mother. Steve listened patiently as I explained my desire to be at home, at least for the first several years, so that I could firmly root the baby in our love and in the love of Jesus. I wanted to be there for his first step, his first words. I wanted to feed him his first jar of Gerbers solid baby food. I wanted to teach the baby the songs and stories of his Lord every day, at all times of the day.

Steve, looking at the practical side of the issue, began to mentally balance our monthly bills against his solitary income. We talked, we planned, we figured, and soon we felt confident that the Lord would be pleased with our decision: I would stay home with the baby.

In the sixth month of my pregnancy, with far less nostalgia than I had expected, I received an honorable discharge from the United States Navy after serving for almost five years. We celebrated that evening with dinner at the Officer's Club and topped it off with one of my favorite desserts—a mint chocolate chip hot fudge sundae.

At the beginning of the eighth month of my pregnancy we signed up for a Lamaze class at Castle Hospital in Kailua, where our baby was to be born. Then we waited . . . and waited . . . and waited. Every day beyond the due date seemed like a month. Talk about grouchy! Finally, early in the morning of May 8, labor began. When I told Steve, "This is it," he asked, "How far apart are the contractions?"

"Seven to eight minutes," I said.

He came back with, "Then it can't really be it because the book says that they have to start at twenty minutes apart."

I wanted to slug him. I couldn't believe he was so regimented by the Marine Corps that he insisted on going by the book even when I was in labor. Three hours later I was in the hospital, and my contractions were two and three minutes apart. They stayed that way for the next thirteen hours. Unfortunately, the baby was turned the wrong way. Several times the doctor tried to turn it, which only increased my discomfort. I couldn't understand why he just didn't leave me alone. After every attempt to adjust the position, it felt like the baby was trying to get back down to its original position all in one contraction. In Steve's exhaustion he said, "I'll never put you through this again."

"Ha!" I snapped back. "That's an understatement, buster! Not to mention that that's *my* line, and I want the satisfaction of saying it!"

Steve was a great coach, though, and that evening we delivered a healthy baby boy, whom we named Steven Louis Bartalsky III. Our miracle baby. The next day was Sunday —Mother's Day—and at church that morning Steve accepted a bouquet of roses in my place.

Five days later Steve was on the airplane to the Philippines to meet his ship while Lil' Steven and I got to know each other.

3
Christina Joan

Daddy saw his son next when he was almost six months old. Steve's face filled with joy as he studied the baby —his very own son. The following eight months were full of countless happy times as we learned to live together as a family. We loved to go out in the evening just before the sun went down and take long walks with Steven in his stroller, his proud father pushing him. Steve took great pleasure in helping to feed Steven, to bathe him, and even to change his diapers. I loved watching Steve with his son. Gentle and caring as a husband, so too was he gentle as a father. Whenever he was home, he spent his energies preparing his son to be President, pitch in the World Series, or win the coveted Pulitzer prize for world peace.

Steven was a perfect baby. He slept through the night, had a healthy appetite, charmed the ladies, and developed through the stages of infancy at an incredible rate. Steve and I couldn't have been happier as new parents.

We felt so privileged to have Steven that the idea of our having a second child to keep the family growing was a welcome one. So when we heard in November that Steve's sister, Elizabeth, was pregnant and wanted to give her baby up for adoption because she was not married, we talked about the possibility of our adopting her baby. We didn't know how wise a decision that would be, and we didn't want to jump ahead of God's will for our family—after all, we had just become first-time parents six months earlier, and Liz's baby would be only ten and a half months younger than Steven —but the idea tugged at us. We prayed and talked the matter over at great length and eventually decided to call Liz and ask her if she would be willing to allow us to be the adoptive parents.

Liz listened carefully but didn't give any indication of how she would decide. She said that she would seriously consider it and call us back in a few days. That was the tough part. I understood the importance of the decision, but I hated waiting. I did my best to leave it in God's care, and, true to her promise, Liz called us back within the week. Her voice was cheerful, and she told us that she felt quite confident that we would give her baby a happy home.

The next few months of waiting seemed ten times more agonizing than the waiting period for Steven's birth. Liz had planned initially to fly to Hawaii and live with us until after the delivery. We had begun to prepare a room for her in our condo, and I had called my gynecologist to set up an exam for her. No sooner had we made those plans, however, than Liz called and told us that she would feel more comfortable in her sister Margaret's home in Fort Lauderdale, Florida.

At first I was greatly hurt by her decision. I wanted to prove to Liz how much I cared for the baby and for her. But I knew that everyone was trying to make the right decisions for everyone involved, and Liz's decision to stay with her sister was clearly the wisest for her emotional well-being. Still, my emotions were shaken. I was afraid that Liz would change her mind about our adopting the baby. Florida was so far away from Hawaii. As much as I hated to admit it, I wasn't trusting the Lord. I was fighting to keep my direct influence rather than just see this as an opportunity to surrender my struggles and rely on the sovereignty of God's will.

Early one morning, about a month before the baby was due, I sought God about my fears. I understood the problem

30

clearly with my mind. It was that I mistrusted God's plan for my life. But gaining peace in my heart and emotions was more difficult. As I read the story of Job in the Bible, God's Word began to make an important promise clear to me, bringing me hope that the emotional roller coaster I had been on would be coming to an end: "He knows the way that I take; when he has tested me, I will come forth as gold" (Job 23:10).

I meditated on this Scripture passage for hours, trying to learn how it applied to my life. The concept of being purified through the fires reminded me of a lesson I had learned as a dental technician in the navy. As I helped dentists prepare for the Hawaii State Dental Exams, I noticed that the stress they experienced was intense and easily frustrated their efforts to perform some of the more tedious stages of the exam. Yet patience was critical to their success. At one stage of the exam the dentists had to fill a tooth with a gold filling. But before doing that, they had to completely purify the gold through fire so that no particle of dirt remained in the metal. If a minute particle were left, the precious metal would not fuse to the tooth; the procedure would be a failure, and the dentist would automatically fail the exam.

Depending on its quality, some gold had to pass through the fire more often than others, and the purifying process could be extremely time-consuming. Each time, as the gold was being heated it was beaten, forcing engrained particles to the surface, and taken to extremely high temperatures to separate the dirt particles from the metal. After the gold had cooled the process was repeated again and again until no trace of dirt could be detected.

Now, in my first fire as a committed Christian, God was telling me that He was just beginning that purifying process within me. I immediately thought, *Why do I get the feeling that this isn't going to be easy?* He knew "the way that I take" because He had created me and had a purpose for His creation. He saw far beyond what my limited eyes of understanding could see. If Liz's baby wasn't to be a part of His plan for my life, then there was a divine purpose in that. Just as gold is tested through the fire, so God was testing me to purify me.

In its weakened condition and permeated with dirt particles the gold was of little value to the dentist. But when it was purified it was extremely valuable. My attitudes were the dust particles that hindered me from accepting God's perfect will for my life, and those attitudes were ingrained in me. I wanted to live up to the challenge of God's will, and I desired to be worthy of His eternal plan, but I needed to undergo a purifying process before He could make me into the image of His Son. In the end, the Scripture promised, I would "come forth as gold."

The final steps for the gold, once purified, were molding and fusing. Those steps had to be carried out with painstaking delicacy to assure that the gold matched the anatomy of the tooth perfectly so that the mouth could function with maximum efficiency. My greatest potential for use in His kingdom would begin once I had been molded and fused to the likeness of Christ. In the years that followed, I was to see the Lord working through heartache to mold and strengthen me as I depended on His promises through many fires. But in the months before Liz's baby was born, I was learning to trust God in that first fire of purification.

Two days before the baby was due, I flew from Hawaii to my parents' home in Sarasota, Florida, to await its arrival. Steven remained with his daddy at home, and I promised Steve I would call the minute I heard news of the baby's birth. From all outward appearances, Steve was in control of any anxiety or emotions about becoming a father again, but secretly I knew he was praying for a girl.

Of course the baby was late, and again each day seemed to last a month. Each night I lay awake trying desperately to surrender the outcome to God. Would she change her mind? Would she decide to keep the baby? *It shouldn't matter*, I told myself. *God is sovereign*. Then I realized how selfish I was. God was bringing more dirt to the surface for purification.

On March 23, 1983, Christina Joan was born. Her middle name, Joan, was chosen so that she would always know that her birth mother loved her deeply, for it was Liz's middle name as well. Two days later Liz presented Christina to me. She was beautiful. As I looked into Liz's eyes and then down at Christina, I sensed the strength and love in Liz's decision, and I admired her deeply for her courage in following through on such a difficult choice. It cost her a great deal, but she knew in her heart that it was right.

Three days later Christina and I boarded a plane to Hawaii where her new daddy and big brother were waiting to meet her. Christina was a darling baby, and we fell in love with her immediately. She seemed healthy, and everyone told us that we now had a millionaire's family: a firstborn son and a beautiful daughter. We were living in a lovely condominium overlooking the rich blue water of the islands, Steve was up for promotion to major in the Marine Corps, and I was working part-time as the Sunday school director at the church we were attending. Life couldn't have been more perfect. I adored my husband, I loved my kids, and my days were filled with the activities of the Lord's work. This was the happily-ever-after that you dream of on your wedding day.

That serene life-style was to last only a few weeks.

Our troubles began with a small, but nagging, difficulty any parent would have with a newborn. Even though Christina looked healthy she seemed to throw up her food quite often, and when I took her in for her first regular check-up when she was fourteen days old I asked the doctor how normal that was. He suggested that we chart her input and output each day and watch her weight very closely.

When one week had gone by and she still had not gained any weight, the nurse suggested that we change formulas. When that didn't work, she suggested that we make the formula heavier by putting baby cereal in it. She also suggested that we sit Christina up between every two ounces for ten minutes before burping her. We finally reached the point where I was going into the clinic twice and sometimes three times a week to check her progress. If she gained an ounce or two in a week, everyone was pleased.

Within a month, we were weighing her food down so heavily with the cereal that we had to cut a big gouge in the nipple of the bottle in order for her to suck the food. We would feed her about a quarter of an ounce, sit her up for a while, burp her, and then start all over again. It was a long, tedious, and time-consuming job, and there were times when I got angry because it made so great a demand on my time.

Then trouble came from another quarter. One day Steve came home with the news that he had been passed over for promotion to major. If he didn't make it the next time, he would be forced out of the Marine Corps. Steve called Marine Headquarters in Washington to find out why he had been passed over, and he asked what he could do to increase his chances at the next promotion board.

The answer from Washington was that he didn't have high enough ratings with his peers, that he needed more administrative experience, and that he didn't have enough sea time. We asked the Lord, "What should we do? If You want us to stay in the Marine Corps, You'll have to show us what to do."

We had only one year left in Hawaii, and Steve had already completed two six-month cruises during the time we had been there. Could we fit in another cruise? Would the Marine Corps let him go on such a cruise? In addition, we had decided that we needed to sell the condominium, and that would be difficult to do with Steve out in the middle of the ocean somewhere.

What could we do but trust the Lord?

In the next few weeks, two important things happened. First, Steve received a letter of commendation from the general of the air station for successfully reorganizing the Classified and Secret Materials Section of the Air Wing's Group Headquarters Division to operate under maximum security standards. Second, a colonel friend approached Steve with an

34

offer that appeared to come straight from the throne room of God. The colonel asked Steve to come over to his squadron and become the administrative officer for a six-month cruise beginning three months later. The administrative position was actually considered a major's billet, and it would enable Steve to receive higher ratings with his peers.

While we sat on the bed one afternoon, Steve and I had a long talk. We agreed that if God wanted us to stay in the Marine Corps, the colonel's offer would be perfect for resolving every problem the Marine Corps had designated. So we put the condo on the market and prepared to move into military housing for our final year in Hawaii. The house sold when Christina was three months old.

Christina seemed to reach a turning point about that time. In a week and a half she gained one pound four ounces, the nurse at the clinic was not demanding that we bring Christina for examination so often, and the rough days appeared to be over. One friend was finally able to draw a good belly laugh from Christina that made my heart jump and my eyes sparkle as I watched them playing on the floor. She was going to be OK.

One Saturday, we decided to shop for new carpeting for our house on the base. We had to drive over the mountain from our condo to Honolulu. Christina seemed particularly irritable, especially when we made turns in the car or stopped quickly in heavy traffic. But we didn't think too much about it and returned home late in the afternoon.

That evening, Christina started to throw up her meals again. We thought we were in for a repeat of her earlier feeding problems and decreased the amount of food we gave her between burpings. The next day she was listless. I was worried and called the emergency room to see if a pediatrician was on duty. None was, and I knew that the general practitioners on duty were especially critical of "nervous mothers" who called or wanted to come in on the weekends, for they didn't have to stay at the clinic if there were no patients. Some of the doctors tended to be sarcastic and rude with the mothers, especially if they were not pediatricians and not used to working with small children. I knew I wouldn't get much help until Monday, so I put Christina on a clear formula, which helped stop dehydration.

I put Christina to bed that evening, but a few hours later, I heard small sounds coming from her room. It sounded like she was whining and having a bad dream. When I picked her up, she acted annoyed by the movement. She felt warm, and I took her temperature. It was a little high—about 99 degrees—so I gave her some aspirin, took her downstairs, and gave her something to drink. I was concerned because these were not her usual symptoms. I called the clinic again, but no doctor was on duty. The corpsman agreed with everything I was doing and suggested that I bring her in first thing in the morning.

I laid Christina on the couch, sat down on the floor next to her, and stayed up most of the night watching her. When morning came, I got her and Steven ready to go, and we drove to the clinic. In the car on the way there, I felt Christina's head again, and her fever seemed to be higher than it had been when we left. She was still irritable when I moved her, and I distinctly remember thinking that the problem had something to do with her back or neck. She hated to be shifted. I had been to the clinic so often in the past three months with Christina that I didn't understand why I felt so nervous.

I took Steven to the babysitter's first and then went to the clinic. The corpsman took her temperature. It was up to 104 degrees. She told me to sit in the waiting room. They would call me soon. Christina sat in her little infant seat in front of me, and I watched her, my heart pounding with uncertainty. She was totally helpless, and there was nothing I could do to help her. She started to whine again, and I couldn't take it anymore. I began to cry.

I kept going back to the corpsman. "How much longer?" All she could say was "You are next." A few minutes later a flight surgeon I knew from church choir walked by and saw me, and I told him what was wrong. He felt the soft spot

36

on top of Christina's head and quietly commented, "This is one sick little girl." That scared me so much I began to sob. All the mothers with their own sick little babies were staring at me, but I didn't care.

The corpsman walked by me once more, and I pleaded to know how much longer. Seeing how distressed I was, she said she would check. I had been sitting in that waiting room for more than an hour—but when they finally called me into the doctor's office, he couldn't move fast enough. He called Tripler Medical Center, told them I would be coming at once, and to please meet me in the emergency room.

We rushed to the clinic's emergency room. There, the doctors started an IV on Christina, and I called Steve at work. Through my tears I tried to tell him what was happening. Then Christina and I were thrust into an ambulance and sped over the mountain to the hospital. While I sat in the back with Christina, the young attendant talked to me and tried to get my mind off what was happening. But that was difficult. I could hear the sirens of the ambulance and Christina whimpering, and as I looked out the rear window I could see cars pull back slowly onto the roadway as we sped by. A sense of urgency overwhelmed me and I felt no control as I was being swept along by the circumstances.

4
A Little Ambassador

We finally got to the emergency room of Tripler Medical Center, and a doctor whisked Christina out of my arms and headed down the hall as I ran after her. Trying to keep up, I asked the doctor if she knew what was wrong, because the doctor at the clinic hadn't told me anything. She replied gravely that she suspected spinal meningitis. I didn't fully understand what that meant. I pressed further: "Is she going to be OK?"

"I don't know," she said, trying to catch her breath.

For the first time the thought of losing Christina penetrated my heart. *What do you mean you don't know? Of course she's going to be all right!* Until that moment, I had never suspected she wouldn't be OK. Suddenly I had to face a whole new reality.

Steve arrived shortly afterwards, and we waited together for the doctors to tell us something . . . anything. The day shift began to go home, and the corridors seemed long, dark, and desolate. Finally, the doctors came. The doctor who had met me in the emergency room confirmed to us that Christina did have spinal meningitis and that during the day she had gone into a semi-comatose state. She was so fragile from her weight gain problems that she had very little with which to fight the disease. The meningitis was rapidly consuming her.

39

So that they could care for her better, the doctors had taken her to the Coronary Care Unit. When next we saw her, she was lying on a big bed with tubes and machines all around her. The doctors tried to be encouraging, but I could see the words "serious condition" written on her chart. I had worked in the medical profession long enough to know that that was not encouraging.

Before we left the hospital we called our immediate family to tell them about Christina's condition, but the person we were most concerned about was Liz. When we told Steve's dad, he said that he would call her because she was still at work. Liz came home right away and together she and Mary, her stepmother, looked up spinal meningitis in the home medical book. She read all of the symptoms of the disease, which were identical to Christina's ongoing condition for the last three months. If the disease is not diagnosed early, the book said, 90 percent of the cases are fatal. Liz read the words in tears.

The doctors suggested that we go home and try to get some rest. There was nothing else we could do at the hospital. Steve agreed, and he took me home, but I was still very distressed. Was there something obvious I should have seen sooner? What could I have done to prevent this? Why did the symptoms of spinal meningitis have to be identical to the problems she already had? Could she possibly have had the meningitis for so long without its being detected? I desperately needed to be held up in prayer.

That night my monthly prayer group met. Steve wanted me to go. In the meantime he would pick up Steven, who was still at the babysitter's.

When I arrived at the meeting and told everyone what was happening, all the women prayed for Christina and me. It was good to be surrounded by familiar faces lifting up prayers to God. It felt normal. The speaker that night—who didn't know who I was or the fact that it was my Christina in the hospital—spoke to my heart. She talked about how God truly desired to bless each one of us.

"Do you really believe that?" she asked.

She asked different people to stand and then personally challenged them with the same question. When she got to me, she simply said, "Do you know that God wants to make you an object of his kindness?"

I knew at that moment that I had to trust Christina to God and decide whether I believed the words of Romans 8:28: "We know that in all things God works for the good of those who love him, who have been called according to his purpose."

As I drove home from the meeting, I began to sob uncontrollably and cry out to God. I hurt so much inside I didn't see how I could live with the pain in my heart. I wanted Jesus *right there*. I wanted His peace. And I wanted the pain to go away. I cried out in anguish and prayed aloud through my tears all the way home. I don't know exactly what I said to God that night, but when I woke up the next morning to a phone call from the hospital, I knew that Jesus had heard my cry and had answered me. I felt peaceful. The desperation was gone.

The voice on the other end of the line said, "You had better come right away. We don't think that Christina will make it through the day." After taking Steven to the babysitter's, we rushed to the hospital to find that she was no longer breathing on her own—she had been put on life support systems. They also had put her on a machine that calculated the pressure of fluids in her head. She had tubing and wires coming from every part of her body. She looked hideous.

We had brought her favorite blanket and a little white lamb that played "Jesus loves me," and we stayed with her until late in the night. She had made it through the day, but the doctors said that if she recovered, she would have irreversible brain damage.

Many of our friends came to see us and comfort us while we were at the hospital. These dear people poured out their love and concern. They hugged us, prayed for us, brought us food, ran errands, or just sat in silence. It was a day for truly understanding what it meant to rest in His love. Yet I still longed to see what the meaning of Christina's illness was, wanted to see why God was putting us through this purifying fire. I sensed that the Lord was going to allow Christina to go to her heavenly home. Why, I don't know, but I believe that God in His mercy was preparing me to accept His will.

Very early the next morning the hospital called and told us to come immediately. It was hard to believe that only forty-eight hours had passed since I had taken Christina to the clinic. We got ready, dropped Steven off at the baby sitter's, and raced to the hospital. There we faced another wait. Christina had been taken for a CAT Scan that probably would take forty-five minutes.

More than two hours went by—and still no word. Did the nurses know if anything had gone wrong? They called the X-ray room and learned that the electrical power had gone out just as Christina's X rays were being processed. The technicians had tried to retrieve them from the developing machine using the hospital's emergency generator power but were unable to do so.

By the time Christina was brought back to the CCU, the X-ray crew still was unable to recover the X rays. Later we found that the electrical power had gone out on the entire leeward side of the island. I'm sure technical reasons could be cited for the power failure, but I believe there was a spiritual one as well. God was allowing Steve time to work through a decision the doctors had begun to place before him. There had been talk earlier of taking Christina off the life support systems that kept her body functioning. But Steve was not comfortable with such a choice. Within the past six weeks one of the priests at the Roman Catholic church he attended had given a sermon on euthanasia. The message was clear: "You are never to pull the plug no matter what the circumstances." Steve was not one to argue with a man who had given his life over to religious service, and the sermon made a strong impression on him. Yet he had absolutely no peace with the idea of Christina's being hooked up to machines just to keep her functioning physically, for it was obvious by that time that our little Christina was no longer in the lifeless body that lay so still. We could see that, and so could the medical staff and our friends.

If the results had come back from the CAT Scan that day, the doctors would have been able to prove that, but the information would also have forced a decision on removing Christina from the machines before Steve had come to peace of mind on the subject. If he had had to make the decision then, he might always have been haunted by the thought that his decision had taken her life prematurely. God in His wisdom and tenderness understood that Steve needed the time to work things through in his own mind and heart, and in mercy allowed Christina Joan to make it through another day.

On Thursday, we asked our chaplain to come and perform a service of dedicating Christina to the Lord. We invited many of our friends, and we all gathered in the staff lounge next to the CCU. We held hands, we cried, we prayed, and we sang to the Lord, asking that His glory be revealed. It was a beautiful service, and once again I felt tremendous peace. The verses of Philippians 4:6-7 came to mind: "Do not be anxious about anything, but in everything, by prayer and petition, with thanksgiving, present your requests to God. And the peace of God, which transcends all understanding, will guard your hearts and your minds in Christ Jesus."

Steve and I talked after the service, and we both clearly believed that the Lord had spoken and had touched us with the assurance of His love. We knew that He was going to take Christina home. I told Steve about the stages God had taken me through before I could finally accept that. At first, when Christina went into a coma on the night we brought her to the hospital, I thought, *I know she will have brain damage, and God will have to show me how to handle that; but as long as she can come home, that's OK.* On the following morning, the doctors said we might be able to take her home even though her condition would only decline, with the machines supporting her until she slowly passed away, and I thought, *OK Lord, if this is what you want, I know you will give me the strength and love I will need to endure this.* And then I had to accept her death. Somehow, through the mercy of God, it did not overwhelm me. I knew that I had accepted it sometime Tuesday afternoon when all our friends were there expressing their love. In being able to accept the fact that she was dying, the burdensome fear of the unknown lifted. God had a purpose in bringing her to her heavenly home so soon, and somehow what we were experiencing fit into His plans for bringing the hearts of men closer to Him.

Thursday afternoon Christina's condition grew steadily worse. By that time she had been comatose for three days and was totally unresponsive. Her body was entirely overwhelmed by the bacteria in her spinal fluid. We could only wait to see how long she could maintain her bodily functions on the life support systems.

It was not that we didn't pray for healing. We did. Yet God was stretching our faith so that we could trust him with full sovereignty in our lives.

That evening a couple we hardly knew came to visit us. They were known to have the "gift of healing." Neither Steve nor I had any question regarding God's ability to heal: "Is any one of you sick? He should call the elders of the church to pray over him and anoint him with oil in the name of the Lord. And the prayer offered in faith will make the sick person well; the Lord will raise him up. If he has sinned, he will be forgiven" (James 5:14-15). We had been praying for Christina with several pastors and friends all week long. It is natural to want to pray for healing and restoration. But when the couple came in, they seemed able to focus only on healing and not on the growth God can bring about through suffering. They asked us what we thought God was telling us. But when we began to describe for them the events of the week and the transformation that had occurred in our hearts, they seemed almost impatient to get to Christina and "operate their gift."

They began to pray, and Steve and I joined them. Their prayers got louder and louder until they were almost shouting in the Coronary Care Unit, in spite of the fact that the people in that area were seriously ill. They began to demand this and command that and invoke God's healing in the name of Jesus. They went on for more than an hour until Steve sat down on a little metal step stool in the corner of the room, put his head between his hands, and stared at the floor. I could feel confusion rising up within me as well. Had God really been speaking to us? Didn't Steve and I have faith enough to pray those same prayers? Was it our fault and because of our lack of faith that Christina was in the condition she was? The conflict in my heart was raging. Until that evening I believed I had heard from God, and He had confirmed it by telling Steve the same thing separately. *So what* is *it, God? What are You trying to teach us?* I asked.

Then I remembered my friend Patty. She walked with the Lord in quiet steadiness. She would be able to look at our situation more objectively than we could. But how could I get in touch with her? I went to over to Steve and knelt in front of him. For a while we held hands in silence. About twenty minutes later a nurse came in to tell me that I had a phone call. I followed her to the nurses' station, and when I picked up the phone, it was Patty. How wonderful God is! I told her in a shaky voice what was happening and explained that the couple had been praying over Christina for more than an hour and that both Steve and I were doubting our own faith. Their prayers were causing discord in our hearts and uneasiness in the hospital staff, who had other critically ill patients to care for near Christina. Gently and with the authority only a true friend could command, she said, "Kathy, what is God telling you?"

I felt a shudder of relief as I told her of God's dealings in both Steve's and my heart. God was preparing us to accept Christina's death. Once again, as I rested in what I believed to be God's plan for us, I sensed His love, and it began to wash out the confusion and unrest in my soul. I went over to Steve and said with renewed hope that Jesus is always faithful to calm the raging storm. After I had told him of my phone conversation with Patty, we both recognized that God was asking us to trust His voice in our hearts as an intimate, personal, and distinct word of comfort to us, because He cared about the circumstances and needs of our lives.

> Turning your ear to wisdom and applying your heart to understanding, and if you call out for insight and cry aloud for understanding, and if you look for it as for silver and search for it as for hidden treasure, then you will understand the fear of the Lord and find the knowledge of God. For the Lord gives wisdom, and from his mouth come knowledge and understanding. (Proverbs 2:2-6)

We believed that the couple who had come to pray with us in the Coronary Care Unit had come with sincere hearts, desiring to help and encourage us. But we also believed that God does not always choose to heal in the physical realm. When we pray for a loved one and healing does not occur, that same faith can be used for the healing of our hearts as the "loved ones left behind." We can still put our hope in God's promises.

On Friday morning, July 15, 1983, the doctors did an EEG to see if they could detect brain activity in Christina. When the reading showed absolutely no response, the doctors told us that she was brain dead. With heavy hearts Steve and I agreed to remove Christina from her life support systems. After the doctors removed all the equipment, they allowed us to come back into the room. There, one doctor gently took Christina from the bed and placed her in my arms. I sat down in a rocking chair with Steve beside me, while our pastor and a close friend, Dan,* joined us. With silent tears I rocked her until her tiny, frail heart stopped beating. It took only a minute or so, but we knew she was now being rocked in the arms of Jesus.

Not more than five minutes later, a nurse came in and took Christina's body away. Our pastor suggested that we go

* Not his real name.

46

down to the hospital chapel and dedicate her to His care. I remember sitting in that chapel with Steve and Dan next to me softly singing "Amazing Grace." Then we sat in silence for a while and listened to God as He began to heal the pain and loss we were feeling so deeply.

Later that day we phoned Steve's parents, who in turn called Liz. Thankfully, God had already prepared her heart before she even received the final word. She had peace in her heart about the death of her daughter. She cried throughout the evening and into the night, but her tears allowed her to release some of the pain she felt.

That night we had dinner at the officer's club with Dan and his wife. After we finished eating, we walked to the top of a hill overlooking the bay. We could see in every direction. The lights from the yachts in the harbor sparkled on the water, blending on the horizon with a clear sky full of stars. We sat down to take in the beauty and the quiet and to reflect.

Dan wasn't a Christian and had been questioning Steve and me about God all week. That evening he told us how helpless he had felt throughout our ordeal. He knew he had absolutely no power to offer us any hope. After eight years of training in medical school to learn how to save lives and after scarching in the years since for the answers to man's problems, there was still a void. He had never thought that he could believe in God or that he needed God, but after watching Steve and me draw upon God's strength all week, Dan decided that he wanted to know Him as well. We talked at length about the redemption of Christ and about God's desire that all men come to know Him. Dan anguished over the fact that it took the death of a tiny baby to open his eyes to the love of the God who created him. Yet Steve and I rejoiced in the news. The death of Christina had worked in Dan's life to bring him closer to an understanding of who God was. It had laid a foundation of the knowledge of Christ in the heart of a full-grown man. Christina's death was not in vain. She had been a little ambassador for Christ here on earth.

5
Colby Matthew

The week after Christina's death we moved out of our condominium and into our base house. Moving was a good diversion. It kept us from dwelling on the past and helped us shift our focus to the future. Christina's memorial service was held four days later at the Kaneohe Marine Corps Chapel. Many of our friends came, along with several of Steve's peers from the helicopter squadron. She was buried in the Pali Valley below majestic mountains, her gravestone proclaiming that she was "Chosen for Glory."

Steve and I had heard the promise of Romans 8:28 often: "We know that in all things God works for the good of those who love him, who have been called according to his purpose." Now it was time to pick up the pieces and trust God for His glory.

A month passed, and Steve prepared to go out on his next six-month deployment. Those planned separations were hard and, for me, emotionally draining. Before he left, we tried to convince ourselves we could live without each other, but that only caused us to build up walls. We picked on each other and fought about unimportant things. If Steve was late getting home from work, I got upset and started thinking he didn't love me anymore. He, in turn, would give the house a "white glove inspection." One day when I left the kitchen cupboard doors hanging open, he acted as if I should have been up for court martial. I guess we thought that if we were mad enough at each other when he had to leave, neither one of us would care that the separation was finally occurring—we'd imagine that life would be better as a result of the distance between us.

We had about five weeks left in our emotional boxing match when one morning I received a phone call from the attorney who had handled Christina's adoption. He said that he had been thinking about us all morning and, as he had before, expressed his sincere condolences about Christina. I thanked him, but I knew that wasn't what was on his mind. He went on to say somewhat cautiously that he had just received a phone call from the local hospital. A baby boy had been born that morning. It was before his due date, and he was up for adoption. Since he was early, a family had not yet been assigned to him. Did we want him?

Did we want him? My heart did a flip-flop, but I tried to maintain some degree of control as I answered, "I will have to ask my husband. Can I call you back?"

"Yes, but I need to know pretty soon, so please don't be long."

I was excited but nervous about calling Steve. A baby! What would he say? What should we do? I called Steve at work, and there was no mistaking his astonishment. How could we make such a decision so quickly? He replied, "Well, I'll have to pray about it, but Kathy, I have to leave in about six minutes." Pray! Of course, we had to pray!

I said, "OK, honey, but pray about it now because the attorney said he needed to know rather quickly."

"All right, I'll call you right back," he replied with growing excitement.

When the attorney had called, I had been lying on the living room floor reading my morning devotions. The two passages I had just read were in the books of James and 1 Timothy:

50

Every good and perfect gift is from above, coming down from the Father of the heavenly lights, who does not change like shifting shadows. (James 1:17)

For everything God created is good, and nothing is to be rejected if it is received with thanksgiving, because it is consecrated by the word of God and prayer. (1 Timothy 4:4-5)

When I got through talking with Steve I went back to my Bible, and this time the words leaped off the page. I was so excited I could hardly sit still as I waited for Steve to call. I knew this child was going to be a gift from God. Not even two minutes passed before Steve called to say, "Honey, if this child needs a home, we have one to offer him." I'm sure I responded in a mature fashion—like screaming into his ear. My thoughts raced. *A baby! We are going to have a baby! Oh dear! I have two days to get ready! What should we call him? Praise the Lord for such a beautiful husband!*

I called the attorney back, and he said we could pick up the baby as soon as the mother was discharged from the hospital. I also learned that the baby was born in the same hospital in which our son Steven had been born and that he had been delivered by the same doctor.

Two days later, on August 25, 1983, I went to the hospital to find a blond-haired, blue-eyed baby boy. He had a funny-looking little face from the struggle of being born, but I loved it. Steve and I thought about many names, but we decided on Colby Matthew because of its dual meaning. Colby means "honored man" (because we felt that he had been honored by God to be brought into a Christian home), and Matthew means "gift of Jehovah" (because we believed that he was a very special gift from God to our family). Everyone was shocked but thrilled to learn that we had a new baby in our home so soon after we had lost our daughter. I'm sure that some people thought it was *too* soon or that we were trying to replace Christina with Colby, but that wasn't it at all. We sim-

51

ply thanked God for His mercy and His willingness to allow us to care for little Colby.

When we went to church that Sunday, I took Colby in his infant seat up to the front and placed him between the organ and my seat in the choir pew. Before the service, the chaplain walked over to me and asked me if I had any announcements to make concerning the Sunday school (I was still its director). As he asked me, he studied the baby very intently. He knew the organist had had a baby about a month earlier, but I could tell from his face that he knew there was something different about the little one at his feet. I told him that I did have an announcement to make and smiled at him as he went back to prepare for the service.

Just before the offering was to be taken, the pastor asked me to make my announcement. I began by thanking everyone for their prayers and concern. For the benefit of the visitors and new families, and there were always a few, given the military rotation system, I described the day we took Christina to the hospital, and I told them about what the speaker had said that night at the monthly prayer meeting: she had challenged us to believe that God loved us personally and wanted to make us the objects of His kindness. I made announcements almost every Sunday, I told them, but on this particular day I felt like Jeremiah when he cried to the people of Israel, "If I say, 'I will not mention him or speak any more in his name,' his word is in my heart like a fire, a fire shut up in my bones. I am weary of holding it in; indeed, I cannot" (Jeremiah 20:9).

I paused dramatically and then smiled and said, "God has given Steve and me a miracle, and now we would like to present to you our son, Colby Matthew Bartalsky."

With the proud face of a new father, Steve took Colby out of his infant seat and held him up for the people to see. The chaplain flew over to us as the congregation spontaneously broke into applause in praise to the Lord. The chaplain went on and on about how he had "looked at that baby over there by the organist and couldn't quite pick out what was different about it." Steve and I glowed. In that moment the praises of our hearts could have been summed up in the words of an aging king more than a thousand years earlier: "I will come and proclaim your mighty acts, O Sovereign Lord; I will proclaim your righteousness, yours alone. Since my youth, O God, you have taught me, and to this day I declare your marvelous deeds" (Psalm 71:16-17).

Steve and I felt wondrously fat in the mercies of the Lord. We knew we were privileged to be a part of His praises, sharing His joy with His people, who had so spontaneously clapped their hands in worship of His marvelous deed in our lives. "May the peoples praise you, O God; may all the peoples praise you" (Psalm 67:3).

During the next four weeks, we began to adjust to the idea of being a family of four again; and then we prepared to become a family of three, as Steve would shortly be at sea. As usual, the last few days before he left were the most difficult, but fortunately by that point all our walls were down. The reality of being apart and the knowledge that we would miss each other was bigger than the pride in either of us. The ever-so-important "I love you's" were expressed in words and in actions without reservation. Steve tried to resolve business transactions and financial problems so that I wouldn't have to worry about them, and I planned special dinners and time alone with Steve whenever he could sneak away from his increasing responsibilities with the squadron.

During one of those special dinners Steve talked about the status of our financial accounts, and he told me, "If you want to come and visit me this winter in a few of the ports that the ship visits, we can afford the expense." He said that with a perfectly straight face. He might have been saying, "Christmas will be canceled this year." When the magnitude of his statement finally dawned on me, he broke into a smile of triumphant pleasure. He knew he had totally surprised me. We had talked about it before, but as soon as Christina got sick, I had dismissed any thoughts about a trip overseas.

The following day I called my parents and asked them if they would mind coming to Hawaii for a few months and babysitting Steven and Colby for about three weeks of that time. I would go to the Philippines for two weeks over Christmas and then to Hong Kong to bring in the new year with my husband. They agreed, teasing me about how big a sacrifice they would be making to live in "paradise" for so long.

Steve left for sea at the end of September. It took me about three days to realize how much help Steve had been in taking care of the children. Colby was turning out to be a difficult baby—he constantly cried and was hard to please. I wondered if his unhappiness was due to his being torn away from his biological mother. I tried to keep him happy, but many nights he lay awake crying—and I was crying with him because I felt so tired and helpless.

Later, he did seem to settle down a little, but he was always quick to whine and make a face, with his big lower lip protruding under the upper one. One thing about Colby, though—he turned out to be gorgeous. In three months his not-so-handsome birth face blossomed into an adorably cute little charmer. Sometimes when Colby was in one of his crying fits the only things that saved him from my wrath were his beautiful face and deep blue eyes shimmering beneath his tears.

One day when Colby was three and half months old, he developed a fever. It came on quickly, and I took him immediately to see the same doctor who had treated Christina. As he was checking Colby, the doctor became very quiet. He didn't move with the same urgency that he had with Christina, but I knew that something was terribly wrong.

He went over to his desk, picked up the phone, and dialed. While he was waiting, he told me that I would have to take Colby up to the hospital immediately for some tests. A shiver ran straight through me, and a knot began to grow in my stomach. "What's wrong with Colby?" I asked. The doctor didn't want to tell me. He said he couldn't be sure until he had seen the test results, but he suspected Colby had the same thing Christina had. I held Colby closer and just stared at the doctor. *Can this possibly be happening again? What is it, Lord? What does this possibly mean?* While the doctor prepared the paperwork for Colby's tests, I called Patty and told her what was happening. Together we prayed over the phone. I can remember Patty's saying, "Jesus, please let Kathy sense Your presence with her as if You were seated next to her in the car on the way to the hospital." I felt a little better after attempting to look to the Lord but couldn't stop wondering, *What is going to happen to my Colby? What is the purpose of this trial?*

During the ride to the hospital, my mind was filled with fears. I had to force myself to hold my thoughts in check through prayer so that I wouldn't be overwhelmed. When we arrived at the hospital, they sent us straight to the pediatric ward. As I waited at the reception desk to sign in, I grew irritated. *Surely these other babies aren't as sick as mine,* I thought. I wanted to cry, but pride won out. When my turn finally came I asked the corpsman if I could see the same pediatrician who had worked with Christina. Five minutes later Colby's name was called, and, needless to say, the doctor didn't understand what I was doing with a three-month-old baby.

I explained Colby's story to her while she examined him. After a few minutes, she interrupted me and said, "We have to run some tests on Colby. I'm afraid, like Christina, we will be diagnosing spinal meningitis." I received the news in what was probably controlled shock and followed the doctor out of the office.

She took me to a waiting area, and while I was there, the chief of pediatrics came out to talk to me. He knew who I was because he had been in charge of Christina's case. Honestly, I felt that he was more concerned about me than he was about Colby. Sensing that made me feel better. He told me that it was nothing a mother could prevent. There was no immunization shot available at that time, especially for infants. I was deeply thankful for his concern and grateful that he had taken the time to talk to me.

He asked where Steve was, and I told him that he had been gone about six weeks on another float. He looked a little troubled at that and told me I could go to the Red Cross office and send a radio message to the ship as soon as I knew what the results were. Again, I was thankful for his help, but I wasn't sure I wanted to worry Steve when he was out in the middle of the ocean. I knew he would feel helpless and separated.

Two hours later, the doctor came out and confirmed her suspicion that Colby had meningitis. But she had good news: his was not bacterial but viral. That meant that Colby's illness was something like pneumonia, though it was still serious enough for him to be hospitalized. She assured me that they would watch him closely throughout the evening, and if he didn't respond immediately to the medication, they would put him in an oxygen tent. They let me hold Colby for a while before they took him up to the ward.

I went up to the Red Cross office, and they radioed Steve aboard the ship. By the time we got his response the next day, we already knew that Colby was going to be all right. He only needed a few more days in the hospital and a full medicinal treatment. We were able to radio back a good report to Steve, so there was no need for him to return.

I still don't fully understand all the reasons the Lord had me face that trial alone so soon after Christina's death. Even today, I ponder over it and wait for God to reveal what He wants me to learn from it. I believe that God was asking me to increase my trust in Him. I know that through the trial with Colby I was able to release much of the guilt I carried concerning Christina's illness and death. This time God chose to heal my baby. This child got better. This child came home.

6
The Passover

Colby came home from the hospital in three days, and within a week he was playing and crying with all the vitality of normal health. With life returning to a schedule, the next six weeks flew by, heightened by the preparations for Christmas. As the Sunday school director, I was responsible for the children's play, and I ran rehearsals until the script was memorized and could be half-convincingly acted out. The play, *The Star of the Savior*, was my first attempt at writing anything with literary value. Working with the children to bring the story to life was as exciting for me as it was for them.

Amid all of that excitement, I prepared for my trip abroad. Other than my parents' arrival, the play was the only diversion that kept me from exploding with the anticipation of leaving my children for the first time, going overseas, and seeing Steve. Fortunately, the one and only performance of the play was to be held a few hours before my scheduled departure. My mind stayed active, my hands were kept busy, and I put off packing until after the show—just in case I ran out of things to do.

Finally, at 3:00 A.M. on December 20, I left for the Philippines. After thirteen hours of flying, I arrived in Manila with recharged energy, and I eagerly looked for Steve on the other side of the busy, crowded customs booths. Not until I was stamped, sealed, and shuffled through did I catch my first glimpse of him. He had grown a moustache! He looked fantastic! But then he could have grown a goatee (which I despise), and he still would have looked fantastic. (After a day or so, however, I probably would have shaved it off in his sleep.)

He led me out of the hot, crowded airport, and I listened with admiration as he disputed with a taxi driver about the price of the fare. Steve was adamant, and a minute later we were crawling into another taxi. We drove to the Manila Sheraton, where we spent the night, and the next morning took a military van to the port of Olongapo where his ship, the *Bellowwood*, was harbored. The drive to Olongapo opened my eyes to an entirely new world. For almost eight hours we drove through nothing but poverty. The devastation began in the streets of Manila, where we saw filthy shanties and dirty children filling every square inch of space. It continued through the farmlands, mountain roads, and villages of every size until we reached our destination in Olongapo, where the poverty was even more pronounced. The surroundings were similar to the slums of New York City, and the immorality like that of Las Vegas.

We drove onto the U.S. Naval Base, and the contrast was startling. I felt as if I had just gone back to America. All around me I saw technology, fine architecture, officers' housing, and baseball fields. Steve explained each scene as it unfolded before me. Although he was only thirty-two years old, he had been on all but two continents (Antarctica and South America). I soaked up his knowledge, almost jealous because I knew I had led a sheltered life back in the States. I recognized images I had seen on T.V., but now those images were replaced by real people in real life.

Steve and I had been supporting The Fil Am Home for Children, an orphanage in Olongapo that sheltered children fathered by American men, and now he took me there. Every time Steve went to the Philippines, he visited the children in the orphanage, whom he loved. He would come home from his deployments with beautiful pictures of children in their ordinary circumstances—full of illustrated cultural expression. He captured them on film so vividly that I felt as if I were there and knew their innermost thoughts. I wanted Steve to take me to see the children so that I could step into their world and share with them a hug from mine.

As soon as we settled into the officers' barracks where we would be staying, we set out to find a "jeepney," a renovated World War II jeep the Filipinos used as taxis. There were thousands of them in Olongapo, and each one was decorated to reflect the life and personality of its owner. The jeepney that we found was owned by a Catholic man who loved rock and roll. Pictures of various saints, posters of famous American musicians, a crucifix, and faded red tassels lined the entire front windshield. We reached the orphanage in about twenty minutes and were immediately surrounded by children. I felt as if I had stepped into one of Steve's pictures. I didn't know which child to hold first. My initial reaction was to find the babies, and when I did, a compassion I had not known before overwhelmed me.

That afternoon I was privileged to meet Mrs. Dunn, a loving Christian woman who ran the orphanage with a dedication and mercy that challenged me to examine my own heart and increase my vision for world missions. Watching her work in her world with such complete peace, I remembered my thoughts about missions as a teenager. *Oh no,* I had imagined, *if I become a dedicated Christian, God will probably send me to the jungles of Africa.* Now, seeing the great need before me, I realized my selfishness. I saw also that my existence would have a greater purpose if I were willing to do anything that the Lord asked me to do. I felt small and humbled, yet at the same time, I knew in my heart that Jesus was saying, "You, too, can make an impact for Me. You, too, can be My hand of love extended to a world where I am the only hope." From that day forward, a desire to be involved in missions began to bloom in my heart.

Steve and I visited the orphanage one more time, bringing bags of Christmas candy for the older kids. We spent the rest of the holidays visiting tourist attractions and spending money in the open markets. We celebrated Christmas Day in Manila eating a turkey dinner with two other couples from the squadron. The following day, Steve made his way back to the ship and I flew on to Hong Kong to await his arrival two days later.

Hong Kong did not have the effect on me that the Philippines had. It thrived like any other major city; the people simply looked different. I met Steve at a landing pier for liberty boats directly across from the Kowloon Harbor where our hotel was located. Unlike the simplicity of our Christmas day, our New Year's celebration was a gala of bright lights, noise, and activity on every street corner; and the familiar melody of "Auld Lang Syne" pealed forth from barrooms scattered throughout the city.

After three days of exhausting our expense accounts on gifts for each other, we said our farewells on the cold, windy steps outside the hotel entrance. In about two months the separation would be over, but for now I focused my energies on getting home and hugging my two little boys, whom I missed terribly.

Steve returned home in February to find that those two little boys had grown quite a bit. Steven, almost two, surprised his daddy with his developing vocabulary. He could complete a full conversation. Colby, no longer a four-week-old baby, had bulked up to become a six-months-old linebacker-to-be. Quite frankly, he was solid.

The reunion was a happy one, but two weeks later Steve and I had our worst blowup ever. Our marriage had been coasting through three years of ignoring one major problem: we both still worshiped in separate denominations. I would drop Steve off at early mass and go on to the Sunday school building a few blocks away from the base chapel. When I was through, I would drive back to the church for the Protestant worship service, and Steve would remain with me, even singing in the choir.

But Steve was our family's spiritual head, and I knew that we needed to be attending church together—in his church. So when Steve returned from the *Bellowwood* I resigned my post as Sunday school director at the Protestant church. We would be going to church with Steve.

To make the break easier, we chose a Catholic church off base, since the military chapel was host to both Catholic and Protestant services. When we entered St. Thomas chapel, I noticed immediately that there were no statues of saints to whom I would be expected to pray. That was comforting, and as the congregation began to sing familiar praise songs, I thought, *Hey, this isn't so bad.* But when the main speaker, a guest bishop, rose to speak, he brought up *every* single doctrine I objected to. My heart grieved to the point of anger.

By the time I left the service I was outraged. There was no way I could subject myself, let alone my children, to those teachings. Steve had read his Bible completely during the past year. I knew that God had been working in his life and that he didn't believe with a whole heart what the bishop was saying, but Catholicism was all he knew. He was making sure that he had "all his bases covered."

For two days I couldn't even talk to Steve. Then, on a Saturday evening, two nights after the service, Steve and I began to talk as we ate our casserole dinner. I had been praying and had to confess to Steve my objections to some of the doctrines of the Catholic church. "I would hate to think that you believe your mother is suffering in purgatory right now for anything she did or didn't do. Christ died for her sins. He is her Redeemer. He took upon Himself the wrath of the Father for her sins. The Bible says that there is no more wrath for those who are in Christ Jesus. Of course He is constantly stretching us to mold us into the beauty of His Son, but that molding is done out of love. He desires our perfection, and we are able to learn and grow into His likeness under the blanket of His forgiveness."

I wanted to knock down the walls between us so that we could worship in unity. The thought of raising our children in

61

the midst of a heated spiritual battle was horrifying. It was certainly not pleasing to the Lord for us to be more concerned about a denomination than His restoration. I told Steve, "I am angry about this, but I promised God I would go anywhere you wanted to go as my spiritual head, and I know the Lord will give me peace in that obedience. But you are responsible to the Lord for leading this family into scripturally sound teachings and for removing this wedge between us."

Steve's struggle was in his understanding of the truth, and as much as I hated the argument, I hated even more that I was so aggressive about the issue. Why couldn't I just rest and let God change Steve's heart? Yet, whether it was misplaced zeal or godly honesty, I couldn't keep quiet. Steve was raised to believe that the Roman Catholic church was the one true church. How could he leave it? The essence of his fear came out when he asked me, "If I leave the Catholic church, aren't I putting my family in priority before God?"

"Why don't we ask the Lord as a couple where He wants us to worship?" I asked.

Steve let out a heavy sigh, came over to me, and hugged me hard. The war was over, and God was victor.

As I was reading in bed that evening, Steve rolled over and asked teasingly, "So, where are we going to church tomorrow?" I had to laugh. I was blessed to have a husband like Steve. We learned from each other, and where many husbands would have ruled with an iron fist and a closed mind, Steve led our family with an open ear for understanding and growth.

The following morning we went to Calvary Episcopal Church, where the Lord, in His mercy, took us both through a stage of transition. The mass was celebrated every Sunday, as Steve was accustomed to, and in contrast to my fears that it might become ritual, breaking the bread with these believers was like entering the throne room of God each week.

One evening while Steve was on duty for the squadron, I went to a class at the church on church doctrine. In all outward appearances, Calvary Episcopal was similar to a Catholic church, but every questionable theory of doctrine was openly discussed in the class. I left completely satisfied and full of the utmost respect for Father Sarge, who patiently answered all of my questions.

Having finally decided upon a church home, only the distant fear of Steve's promotion board meeting in May concerned us. We knew that Steve had done everything the Marine Corps had required—and more. He had received a special evaluation for the work he had done in logistically preparing his squadron for deployment, he was rated number two out of nineteen captains in his squadron, he had acquired the necessary administrative experience, and he had fulfilled his sea-time obligations. Man's requirements had been met.

We tried to put the subject of the promotion in the back of our minds and to enjoy our times together as a family again. Steve helped in marvelous ways with the boys. He never thought twice about changing a dirty diaper, feeding a hungry tummy, or spanking a rebellious bottom. Every night we all gathered in the boys' room to sing songs and read Bible stories. There were many times when I watched Steve read, a boy under each arm, and thought about the time he read *The Old Man and the Sea* to me as our car sped along a dark desert road four years earlier. Now we were a family learning to grow and to love the Lord.

Steve wanted to do something special with the boys to try to make up for all the time he had been at sea. Different ideas were suggested and tossed out, and he finally decided he would take the boys to breakfast every Saturday morning at a waffle restaurant, so that Mommy could sleep in. That became such a special time for the boys that they began to tease me saying, "You're a girl, so you can't come," and with some prompting from their father, I was nicknamed "Lazy Bones" —a name I could live with in order to catch a few extra hours of sleep.

One sunny afternoon, when I was in the kitchen making Steve's lunch and the boys were down for their afternoon naps, I heard Steve's car coming up the driveway. As he came into the house, I noticed that he was very quiet. Then he walked into the kitchen and said, "I didn't make it. I was passed over." A sharp pain went through my heart. I wanted to believe that it was some sort of bad joke, but when I looked into his face I knew it was the truth. We held each other, silently absorbing everything that it meant. The knowledge that we actually had to leave the Marine Corps and the security it had held for us was devastating, especially for Steve. Our world was being shattered again.

7
In Neutral

As I turned back to the stove to stir the butter that was now sizzling in the frying pan, possibilities began to race through my mind. Was it really true? Could some of the dreams we had discussed in the Philippines about doing missions work be in our future? Could we find the good in what appeared to be a bad situation? In no way did I want to make light of the situation with cliché remarks that did more harm than good. But I did want to encourage Steve, and I knew the ideas were from the Lord.

Attempting to be cheerful, but in a serious tone, I said, "Honey, do you realize that now we can go anywhere the Lord wants us to go? Anywhere!" His face became thoughtful, so I continued with a little more confidence, "Think about it, Steve. Maybe we could go back to the Philippines and work with the people as missionaries." I knew I must have sounded idealistic, but now many options were before us. We both loved the Philippines. We always felt inadequate in the small part we played by giving our donations. Giving money just didn't seem to be enough. Now we might have the chance to do something more practical.

Steve had always been open to whatever God's will might be, and although being passed over was a major setback for him, he began to see that there could be life beyond the

Marine Corps. He had often quoted Psalm 75: "For promotion cometh neither from the east, nor from the west, nor from the south. But God is the judge: he putteth down one, and setteth up another" (vv. 6-7, KJV*). As we ate Steve said, "Maybe God needed to hit me over the head with a two-by-four to get me to listen to Him." I laughed as I pictured God standing over Steve with a huge piece of lumber in His hand and Steve knocked out on the ground with little stars and birds circling about his head. I don't know if God actually hit him or not, but I watched Steve's eyes light up as new hope and restored purpose came to him. It was important for us to see that God was in control.

By the time lunch was over, Steve felt 100 percent better. Of course the pain of rejection is never easy to endure, but at that time many other qualified men were in the same position, and we knew that it was not personal rejection. The military had simply become top-heavy in its ranking structure, and rather than keep the qualified and trained men they already had, they opted to train newer and younger men who were just out of college. As a result, we had to put our trust in God and be secure enough to believe that God had a purpose for our lives outside of the Marine Corps.

That afternoon, another marine wife called to tell me that her husband had also been passed over for major. She was bitter about the promotion board's decision, and nothing I said could convince her that there was life beyond the Marine Corps. "How could the Marine Corps do this?" she cried. She had depended upon that promotion for her security and her status. When we hung up, she was just as angry as she was when she called.

Two months later I heard she had deserted her husband, left the island, and filed for a divorce. I saw a contrast between her reaction and our ability to trust God. In the same circumstances, we had the hope and peace that only Jesus offers.

* King James Version.

The job search began. The Marine Corps gave us six months' notice. Steve diligently prepared a résumé and within several weeks had sent out more than two hundred copies. All but one received a standard response: "Thank you for your interest in our company. At this time we do not have any available positions, but we will keep your resume on file for six months. . . . "

The résumé that did yield a positive response was one he had sent through Intercristo, a Christian placement service. They made us aware of an organization based in Switzerland called Helimission. Steve sent his package immediately, and it wasn't long before the director, Ernie Tanner, called him at work. Steve was ecstatic that Ernie had called him all the way from Switzerland.

Ernie explained to Steve some of the criteria of the mission's work. Helimission is a non-denominational mission that flies helicopters in Africa. It is a support mission to all main-line denominations out on the field. Ernie had a great need for Christian pilots whose hearts were committed to God first and to flying second—pilots who weren't just looking for a way to build up their flight time to get a better job in the States later but who were dedicated to the furtherance of the gospel.

That night, when Steve told me about his conversation with Ernie, I knew it was what we both wanted to do. To think that we could be missionaries in full-time service to the Lord. Could it really be possible?

Jesus said, "Everything is possible for him who believes" (Mark 9:23). That verse is true! But reality soon came knocking. The biggest question we had of Ernie was regarding our financial support. He was quick to write back saying that we would have to raise our own support if we were accepted by the mission. For a family of our size he suggested $1,500 each month for the required three years of service.

When Steve and I sat down to figure out our bills in addition to the support, we came up with a frightening figure far above the amount Ernie had suggested. The mission field seemed farther and farther away. How could we in all honesty ask hard-working people to pay our monthly support and the bills we had already accumulated? We just couldn't. We wrote a few more letters to Ernie, but the light of the mission field had dimmed in our hearts, and for the time being we had to put Helimission on the back burner.

Discouraged, we began to make preparations to move back to the mainland. We packed up our household goods, which the Marine Corps was obligated to store for as long as one year. In October 1984 we left Hawaii.

Steve flew to Tucson to visit his father and look for work in the Southwest, and I flew on to Pennsylvania with the kids to show them to my family. Other than my parents, none of my relatives had met the children yet. While I was out East, Steve and I agreed that I would take a bus down to North Carolina to check on our beach house, which we had leased out before leaving for Hawaii. Colleen, my sister-in-law, agreed to watch the boys for me while I was gone.

When I got to Atlantic Beach, a flood of nostalgia swept over me. Steve and I had met there, and technically the beach house had been our first home. I went to the realtor's office to get the key and then drove over to the house with a friend of mine, Kathi, who was stationed at Cherry Point with her husband. What we found was utterly amazing.

Our house had been rented to a middle-aged couple who liked to fish, and that must have been the only thing they liked to do. They were not home at the time, so we were free to look around—and gawk. The house was disastrous. Absolutely filthy! There was clutter everywhere. The smell of animals permeated the carpet and furniture. Dishes were piled high in the kitchen and scattered throughout the rooms. There were big holes in the ceiling, and cat litter was spilled on the dining room floor. The toilets hadn't been scrubbed since the couple moved in, and the bowls were black. The animals had done their "business" in the upstairs rooms on the carpet. Significantly, a magnet on the refrigerator read, "I hate housework."

Terribly angered, I called the realtor at once. Her daughter answered the phone and said that her mother had gone home. Realizing there was nothing the girl could do, I hung up the phone and resigned myself to seeing the realtor the following day. As I stood there telling Kathi about the conversation, my legs suddenly began to itch. I looked down and saw that I was covered with fleas. I couldn't believe it. This made me so angry I called the realtor's daughter back immediately and told her to tell her mother I wanted to see her *now* and that I would meet her at the office.

Kathi and I arrived at the office before the realtor did. I had to control my tears as I sat picking fleas off my jeans and out of my pocketbook, which I had left open on the dining room table. Over and over I kept praying that the Lord would help me handle the situation in a mature way, so that I could somehow reflect His personality. When the realtor finally came, I told her how horrible our house looked. She mumbled something about stopping by six months earlier and telling them to scrub the toilets, but I could see that she just didn't care. Once I realized that, I asked her what it would take to evict the renters. I told her to do it at once and left the office thanking God for His wisdom.

That night while I lay on my bed I meditated on Scripture to keep my heart in line with His will: "In your anger do not sin; when you are on your beds, search your hearts and be silent. Offer right sacrifices and trust in the Lord" (Psalm 4:4-5).

I knew God was telling me to let go of my anger and trust Him in the situation. I was not to take revenge, for revenge is God's alone. My task was to seek God's priorities for me in the situation. What did God want to work in my heart? Once I understood that, I could act knowing I was in line with His will.

As it turned out, I rented the house beside ours, planning to stay in it while the repairs were being made. Then I took the bus back home to pick up the boys. As I rode to Pennsylvania that day a young marine sat behind me, and by the time we parted in Washington, D.C., he had prayed the sinner's prayer and had met Jesus. So though the condition of the house delayed my trip to Pennsylvania, as a consequence a young man came to know the Lord. We never exchanged names or addresses, but I think about him from time to time and pray that the seed that took root that day fell on good soil.

Once I arrived in Pennsylvania, I called Steve and gave him an update on the situation. We agreed that the best plan was for him to stay in Tucson to look for work and find a small apartment, while I took the boys with me to North Carolina to fix up the house. We settled in and quickly began the task of cleaning what the boys were calling "the stinky house." We had the trash hauled away, the holes in the ceilings repaired, the leaky roof fixed, and the carpets cleaned and aired. The toilet bowls had to be scrubbed and bleached three or four times before they were white again. It took an entire month and cost more than $5,000 in renovation and repair, but at last the day came when I felt comfortable about renting the house out again. The Lord was clearly working, because the man who did most of the repairs became our new renter. He promised to keep the house in better shape than he had found it. That wouldn't be too difficult, but I knew what he meant.

The boys and I packed up once again. This time our ride was going to be a little longer. We were going across the country to Tucson, where Steve was waiting patiently. He now had an apartment for us, and in this way we relocated to Arizona to try to begin a new life and seek God's will for our family.

8
Willing

The drop in income was our first challenge. We went from $3,800 a month to $800 a month. Steve tried desperately to find work using his skills. Time and again something hopeful would come up but then fall through. We decided that I should return to work until he found a job. Leafing through the paper, I saw an ad for an oral surgeon's assistant. Steve helped me to write a résumé, and we sent it. I made no other effort to find work because I honestly didn't believe there were that many qualified oral surgery assistants out there looking for a job.

In a few days I was called for an interview, and although it was hard to wait the next couple of days, I did get the job. Once there, however, I found out how much God had had His hand in the situation and how cocky I had been in my expectations. More than sixty-five people had applied for that job, and one of them even had a doctorate. A plaque on the doctor's office wall provided an important clue as to why I got the job, though. The plaque was from the same dental clinic in Hawaii that I had worked in. I had an identical plaque at home—only the dates were different. He had been the head surgeon in the same Oral Surgery Department where I had been head technician. I believe that God used that common denominator to help me get the position.

Meanwhile, at home, Steve was making a big deal about my getting a job after sending out only one résumé. He had sent out nearly eight hundred. God was taking him through a very difficult time and knew I needed that job to fulfill His purpose in our lives. Psalm 13 was the prayer Steve was praying in his heart during that wilderness experience.

> How long, O Lord? Will you forget me forever?
> How long will you hide your face from me?
> How long must I wrestle with my thoughts
> and every day have sorrow in my heart?
> How long will my enemy triumph over me?
> Look on me and answer, O Lord my God.
> Give light to my eyes, or I will sleep in death;
> my enemy will say, "I have overcome him,"
> and my foes will rejoice when I fall.
> But I trust in your unfailing love;
> my heart rejoices in your salvation.
> I will sing to the Lord,
> for he has been good to me.

Even as he cried that prayer in his heart, he experienced another incredible jolt. He had applied for an administrative job at a remote air base that repaired commercial and military aircraft. Because the base was so remote, he was pretty certain he would get the job. Although he was overqualified, it would be a good job.

We thought it would be wise if we could both work there, so I had sent my application to the personnel department as well. I was offered the exact position for which he had applied. It was so ridiculous we both laughed, and though it was another slam for him, he never once lost his spirit or his desire to trust in Jesus. He just said to me, "Don't you remember the prayer at the farewell meeting for us in Hawaii? Remember the man who prayed for God to shut the doors that Satan would try to open?" I marveled at his patience and his maturity in the Lord, but I think it was at that time more than any other that we both realized that God was asking Steve to place his flying on the altar before Him.

After five months we believed that we had exhausted all the possibilities for Steve in Tucson. So he started to drive to Phoenix on a regular basis and there began the process all over again. It wasn't long before we saw the need to move our family from Tucson to Phoenix.

We put a new résumé together for me, and one Saturday after work I drove to Phoenix. On Sunday I looked for an apartment. That was my choice, for when Steve had chosen our apartment in Tucson, we ended up living in a major disaster area. The emergency room at a major hospital with sirens screaming at all hours was our backyard, and a manure manufacturing company greeted us with its aroma each day, made worse as the heat of the desert sun intensified.

On Monday I went to four job interviews, and that evening I was offered a position as a sales/administrator for a large award and trophy company. Steve and the boys moved to the apartment on Wednesday, and I followed soon after. The move was especially good for Colby because he had been suffering from tonsillitis continually due to the dust of a sand volleyball court outside of our Tucson apartment.

Steve met some men who talked with him about entering the life insurance business. He became interested in the possibilities and began to study for the test that would enable him to acquire a license to sell insurance. A couple of weeks later, he found work selling life insurance, but by that time the financial strain had taken its toll. The expenses of the move had put an immense burden on us. Large payments to the electric company, the gas company, and the water company, plus the first month's rent and our security deposit wiped out everything we had saved. And I was under extreme stress from the responsibility of being the sole provider for the family.

Steve knew that, and I recognized how difficult the situation was for him. Being the only one with a steady paycheck every two weeks helped me to appreciate the feelings of inadequacy I knew Steve had been dealing with during the past eight months as he attempted to find work. I was not an ideal wife, and there were times when I let him know how it was all affecting me.

Steve helped with the household chores whenever he could. Yet when I came home from work tired and grouchy, the knowledge that there was a full evening's worth of laundry, cooking, and dishes to do gave me something to complain about. The stress of penny-pinching also reduced the time that Steve and I had alone together. In Hawaii, we had gone out on a date every Friday night, and one Friday each month we had chosen a nice, elegant restaurant for a more romantic atmosphere. In my spirit I knew he was doing all he could to find work, but my flesh was so tired I had to be careful not to blame him. It wasn't easy.

One night, after we had put the kids to bed, we began to talk about how much we missed our dates. Those times had been so special. They allowed us to separate ourselves from the world to talk and to stay close to the life of the other. As Steve was putting the dishes away he said, "We really should do something about having a special time together again."

"That sounds wonderful," I replied, "but how do we do it? I work all day and teach aerobics two nights a week, and you work most other nights. The nights that we can stay home together are important for the kids."

Steve thought about that and agreed. Putting the last plate in the cupboard he said, "So, if we can't be together at night, we'll do it in the morning. We'll go to breakfast one day a week. You pick the day."

That certainly seemed to be the answer to the problem, although it was difficult enough for me just to get up for work. I was the night owl in the family and Steve the early bird. Getting up early one day of the week was a sacrifice worth making, though, and I knew the Lord was a part of our plan. I truly believe that if each of us had not had a firm relationship with the Lord and if we had not believed that He had our best

74

interests at heart, we would probably have left each other because of the strain. Instead, we learned again the value of communication. Communication and prayer kept us from bottling up wrong attitudes that could have taken root and led to bitterness.

During that time the Lord also spoke to Steve and me repeatedly concerning our tithes and offerings. He brought our attention to verses in Malachi about giving to God:

> "Will a man rob God? Yet you rob me.
> "But you ask, 'How do we rob you?'
> "In tithes and offerings. You are under a curse—the whole nation of you—because you are robbing me. Bring the whole tithe into the storehouse, that there may be food in my house. *Test me in this*," says the Lord Almighty, "and see if I will not throw open the floodgates of heaven and pour out so much blessing that you will not have room enough for it." (Malachi 3:8-10, italics added)

Rob God? Had we really been so bold? So blind? We decided that even in our financial struggle we would do what that passage said. We would test God. Not in a defiant way, saying, "OK God, if You're really who You say You are, we'll tithe and just watch the money roll in." We knew we could not buy God. No one can buy His blessings. No one can buy the Holy Spirit as Simon the magician in Acts tried to do. He was scorned by Paul for that attitude, and we did not want to be so foolish as to mock God in the same way.

No, when we tested God, it was a step of faith. "Lord, we have been struggling for almost a year with our finances. We're living from day to day with anxiety about our bills. We now put this situation completely in Your hands, and to show that we trust You and repent of our lack of obedience in this area, we will tithe and give offerings as You direct us."

Together Steve and I agreed on an amount to tithe and an amount to routinely give as gifts and offerings. Anything above those amounts would be as the Lord further directed.

Our tithes and offerings would be first, but our entire income would be dedicated to what the Lord desired.

As we remained faithful to God, we were more sensitive to the way the Lord was meeting all our needs. I can remember one day when the bills were stacked thirteen high, and I sat down with the checkbook and said, "Lord, You are going to have to do it. You know we want to be good witnesses for You; You know that we are working hard and desire to be responsible Christians. We can only trust You."

I wrote check after check, and when I was finally through, we were left with about $5.00 in our account. Our cupboards had food, we had clothes and a home. God was faithful to supply for all our needs.

As we paid those bills, we recognized that we had gotten into the typical American trap: monthly payments, and lots of them. Somehow, we had to rid ourselves of debt and get out of the cycle of credit. We sought the Lord's guidance and decided that we would sell the beach house in North Carolina. In early July we put our home on the market. Because of the repairs we had done, the house was now quite valuable. The appraisal on the property was high, yet we sold it within a month.

What would we do with our profits from the sale? We began by saying, "Well, we'll pay off this bill and maybe that one, and then we'll put the rest into savings." Then God worked on our hearts, and after a week or so we were saying, "OK, we'll pay off all but this one and maybe that one." But by the time we got the check, we had finally agreed to be totally obedient to God's voice. We gave our tithe and offerings and then joyfully paid off *all* of our outstanding debts.

The burden of bills was lifted, and we praised God for His wisdom in directing us to the financial freedom we now had. It was incredible. The floodgates of heaven were opening. We were still eating out of plastic margarine bowls, drinking from Domino's Pizza cups, and renting the scant furnishings in our apartment, but we could see better and happier days ahead.

In four weeks, the government's one-year obligation to store our furniture would be over. There was no way we could squeeze a three-bedroom house—family room, living room, dining room, and kitchen—into our small two-bedroom apartment, especially not with the baby grand piano that Steve's father had given us as a gift. We needed a house, and the search began. We could afford no more than $450 a month for rent. I had resigned from my position at the trophy shop to take a secretarial position at our church, Biltmore Bible, which only restricted our budget more because I had taken a $200-a-month pay cut. However, my work at the church gave me the opportunity to work with Dr. Whitlow, the pastor, to help supply Third World nations with college curriculum to raise up pastors within those nations. I knew that was far more important to the gospel of Jesus Christ than my selling bowling trophies.

Steve and I looked through countless homes in many areas for one we could afford. The more we looked, the more discouraged we became. The neighborhoods were run-down, they were in bad parts of town, and the homes themselves were in great need of repair. I thought, *Lord, I don't want to bring my kids up in filth like this. Please show us where to look.* We tried looking at homes costing a $100 more a month. But that only allowed us to look at houses with one more bathroom in the same neighborhoods.

One Sunday as I lay on the floor reading the newspaper, I saw a home for $650 a month in an area of town I knew was reasonably nice. The price was steep—$200 more a month than our budget allowed, the exact amount of my pay cut. But when we drove out to look at the house, we fell in love with it. We soon learned that a pastor in Texas owned it and had been praying for a Christian family to rent it. It seemed perfect for our needs. But if we took it, we would have to trust the Lord to restore the amount of my paycheck loss. In our eyes it didn't seem possible—but we prayed, we discussed, we planned. We both believed God was saying yes. So we trusted Him, and not once were we late in paying our rent. Steve always made just enough in sales commissions, and together with the Lord we pulled out of our financial slump. God always took care of our needs. With our furniture out of storage we finally set up "home."

We began establishing friendships and getting involved in church activities. The work I did with Pastor Whitlow was primarily editing and copyediting a four-year theological college program. The program was to be given to any missionary to use in establishing a Bible college in a Third World nation. For me, it was a crash course in Bible school. I read four years' worth of theology material—twice. I do not have a degree to show for it, but God certainly used it, and I have drawn on its resources many times. I am thankful for the experience. But greater things than that came out of our experience in Arizona.

More than anything, Steve loved to fly, yet in those months in Arizona he strongly sensed that God was asking him two important questions: Did he want God's will for himself and his family more than he wanted to fly? And could he be content never to fly again if that was what God wanted? I don't really know what went through Steve's mind as he struggled with those questions, but I know that Steve's heart was sold out to Jesus. Steve had one of the most serving hearts I had ever seen in a man. He served others with love and zeal and never expected anything in return. So why were those questions so important?

What was God trying to teach him, and me? I think the answer is found in God's mercy and knowledge of the future. In His love, He was enabling Steve to understand that if he were ever called to fly for Jesus, he would know God had willed it. He wouldn't be out there flying simply because he loved to fly and happened to know how to do it. He would know that God had ordained it, and God would receive the full glory for it. There would be no question in his own mind whether his love for flying surpassed his love for God.

In truth, God was giving us both a precious gift during that time in Arizona. Through that experience we came to realize that we were willing to be where God wanted us be. What a discovery. We knew for certain that with our whole hearts we desired God's will for our lives. One of the verses Steve claimed during that time helped us to focus our eyes on this truth we now shared: "Trust in the Lord with all your heart and lean not on your own understanding; in all your ways acknowledge him, and he will make your paths straight" (Proverbs 3:5-6).

As Steve and I looked back at the death of Christina, the pain we had felt at the rejection by the Marine Corps, the struggle we had had to unite our faith in God, the financial setbacks, the lessons in tithing, and the realization that one day we wanted to serve Jesus on the mission field, we could see that God had been preparing us for a "passover" into the promised land of a new and more dedicated life with Him.

Steve was still selling life insurance, but the company for which he was working was new and soon went out of business for a variety of reasons. Once again he had to start from scratch. "Coincidently," at the same time Ernie Tanner from Helimission called us again from Switzerland. All he said was that he wanted to speak at our church—but we were tremendously excited. Why was the director of a mission coming all the way from Switzerland, taking a detour through Phoenix, and speaking to a crowd of approximately thirty people at a Wednesday night service? We didn't want to get our hopes up, so immediately we went into prayer.

9
The Call

On January 26, 1986, Ernie Tanner came to Phoenix with a boxful of pamphlets and two films. Since he was speaking that evening at the church where I worked, I remained at my desk until Steve brought him from the airport. Our first introductions were brief, because he had to set up the film projector and speak within fifteen minutes. Steve and I had invited many friends to come and hear him, and although Ernie's sermon and films were challenging to everyone present, they were especially exciting for Steve and me. Most of Helimission's work is in Africa, and their goal in using the helicopter is to reach tribes and people groups in the jungle that have never been able to hear the gospel. They call it pioneer evangelism. We were watching films and listening to Ernie talk about a ministry that was a world away, yet within our reach.

After the service Pastor Whitlow, his wife, Donna, and Ernie, Steve, and I went out to a steak house for dinner. Over dinner Ernie spoke to our pastor, asking what he thought of our going to the mission field, and he told us what the requirements for joining Helimission would entail. I kept very quiet and absorbed the possibilities, although Ernie told us he didn't have any openings at that time.

After dinner, Steve and I took Ernie to our house where he was spending the night. Over the kitchen counter, in the much cozier atmosphere, he and Steve talked about helicopters. In less than an hour, I think they had named every possible rotorwing aircraft in existence. Again I kept quiet and listened. Soon the conversation went back to the mission field. Ernie recounted some of his experiences, such as the time he made the first solo helicopter flight in history across the Sahara Desert. I'm sure he noticed that Steve and I were a rapt audience.

Then Ernie talked about the practical things we could do to prepare for missions. One of the things he showed concern for was the commitment of the wife to the ministry. He said it was very difficult for some pilots' wives who go to the mission field because their husbands fly off into the wild blue yonder every day while they are at home with the children in a foreign country, with few or no friends. That was where I came into the conversation, and I told Ernie I wanted him to understand that I sincerely supported Steve in every way I could. Steve and I explained that we believed the Lord was preparing us for and calling us to missions in some capacity.

Ernie listened with quiet authority, his experience and years in the Lord almost intimidating me. Every once in a while he interjected a comment or asked a question, but soon he was telling us that his first suggestion was that we learn French. "Just learn five words a day," he said. "If you learn five words a day you can learn a language in no time." *That's easy for you to say*, I thought. *Europeans are taught several languages from birth and are better equipped to learn them than we are. We Americans—well, maybe you should have a long talk with my English teacher.*

Ernie's fatigue became evident as we talked through the midnight hour, so we decided to pray and end the evening. As we were going to bed, Ernie said that he might have a position for us in about six months.

The following morning, Ernie and Steve arose early and went to the airport. Ernie's flight was delayed, so he and Steve got some coffee. During the conversation, to Steve's amazement and delight, Ernie said that he had been thinking of a way to bring us into Helimission by April. That was only three months away!

Steve phoned me immediately after Ernie's flight left, and I ran to Pastor Whitlow's office to tell him the news. Africa for Jesus—and we could be there in three months! Pastor shared my excitement, and together we looked up on a world map the four countries in Africa in which Helimission was currently operating. But he brought me down to earth when he mentioned the work that lay ahead in raising funds, packing up the house, selling our belongings, and completing Colby's adoption, which was still in the courts.

A day or so later, during my lunch break, I walked down to the canal near our church to seek the Lord. I had a small Bible with me and read various Scriptures as I walked in the warmth of the midday sun. One passage in particular spoke to my heart: "I consider everything a loss compared to the surpassing greatness of knowing Christ Jesus my Lord, for whose sake I have lost all things. . . . I want to know Christ and the power of his resurrection and the fellowship of sharing in his sufferings, becoming like him in his death, and so, somehow, to attain to the resurrection from the dead" (Philippians 3:8, 10-11).

As I meditated on those words, God seemed to be showing me several things. First, my desire to know Him needed to surpass any desire I had to serve Him on the mission field. I was not to go just because I saw the great need to tell others the truths of His Word. There's enough need here in the States for that. Second, God would supply the "burden" for the people of Africa; my job was to *go*. Yes, the Filipino people seemed more "real" now, but that was because I had been able to visit their country. Africa would become "real" for me when I lived there, and the native warriors, pagan religions, and witchcraft that seemed so distant and threatening would take on immediacy when I actually lived on that great continent. It was as though God was saying to me, "The most important thing is that you simply obey Me. Go because I say so and for no other reason. Kathy, don't you think that if I call you to go, I can also give you a love for those people that is real and from your heart and that that love will only deepen as you live and move among them and see their great need for Me?"

The Arizona sun warmed me as I walked along the calm waters of the canal that afternoon, but it in no way compared to the warmth of His love that I felt in my heart. Of course I was to put no confidence in the flesh, for His ways are not our ways. I had to trust His wisdom, for He could certainly call the right people to the right task. The possibility of Steve's and my going to the mission field and not bringing one soul into the kingdom of God was real, and we would probably get discouraged—maybe even give up and come home—if we went without complete assurance that Africa was where God was calling us to be. It dawned on me that God could be calling me simply to grow closer to Him, rather than to make a great impact on the African people. The important thing was that Steve's and my call to the mission field and our success for the kingdom of God be "by [His] Spirit," not "by might" or "by power" (Zechariah 4:6).

Those truths explained the first Scripture in Philippians I had been meditating upon, but I wasn't clear why the rest of the passage seemed so important. Were Steve and I going to suffer or be persecuted? Were we going to see great miracles and wonders of His resurrection power? As much as I sought the Lord's counsel, no clear answer was forthcoming. I concluded that if those verses came to mind from a human impulse rather than the prompting of God, they would soon fade away and be forgotten. But if those verses were truly "from the Lord," He would show me the answers to my questions when the time was right.

Less than two weeks later, on February 12, 1986, Ernie called. Could we be ready to come to Switzerland by March 4? We thought that was too soon, but we told him we would aim for the first part of April. There were 1,001 details—and we had six weeks to accomplish them.

The number one item on our list was to raise our support. How could we do that in six weeks? We had read stories about missionaries who had taken five years to raise all they needed. Another complication was that Colby's adoption was still in a stage of confusion. We had to have the adoption paperwork completed by the time we left so that Colby could get a passport. A third problem was selling everything we could.

The Lord moved quickly and for His glory. Our church in Phoenix raised half of our support. When I went to Hawaii to complete the adoption, I was able to go to our Hawaiian church family at Calvary Episcopal and tell them about the vision the Lord had given us and about what He had done in our lives. They agreed to support us as well and to pray for our needs.

Steve was back in Phoenix delivering pizza for Domino's. He actually made very good money and even became "driver of the week" his first week. He was also doing all he could to sell our household items and our cars. Shortly after my return from Hawaii, we had a huge garage sale. The most painful part of the day for me was watching the baby grand piano go, and for Steve, selling the beautiful leather couch he had bought before we were married. We comforted one another with the knowledge that they were "hay and stubble" anyway. By the end of the day, we had sold almost everything, including one car. The rest we gave away or put in storage at Steve's parents' house in Tucson. We still had not raised all of our support, but we were trusting God to meet that need.

The following morning was Sunday, and we had to say our farewells to Biltmore Bible Church, Pastor Whitlow, and his wife, Donna. All our friends were there as well as some of our family. Pastor brought Steve and me up to the pulpit, and Steve shared his heart with the congregation, at times unable to conceal his tears of joy.

"The Lord has given each one of us a talent, and just as he gave the three stewards talents, he wanted to see what each one would do with them. Two of them increased their talent and one did not. The two that did, did not work out of fear, but out of love for their master. The Lord has given me a talent to fly helicopters. He has placed a call on my life to use this talent. We are only instruments to help, and we want to do it out of our love for the Master.

"I can't come up with a three-point sermon where all the word endings match, so I will draw on my military experience and use an acronym, DOT.

"Dedication. Love is not always emotional, but it is a decision. Once you receive God's love and return it back to Him, you must show this love through your obedience to Him.

"Obedience. You must listen to the Word and then obey it. No excuses.

"Trust. You must trust that He is going to provide all your needs *and* the needs of those people He's called you to provide for."

The next day was our final full day in Phoenix. We were due to leave at 5:30 A.M. the following morning on April 1. God's perfect timing remained with us until the last possible minute. We had a full day of last minute details to take care of and still had to sell our van. By six o'clock that evening we were exhausted, but with everything else out of the way, we began the task of finding a buyer for our vehicle. We drove to various dealerships throughout northwest Phoenix, and within one hour we had sold our van for a great price. We had twenty minutes to make it back to church where I was teaching my last aerobics class. Ten hours later we were on an airplane to our first destination, Pennsylvania.

Before we could leave for Africa, Steve had to go to Philadelphia for a week to update his flying qualifications. Initially, we stayed at my brother Dave's house in Harrisburg, the same house in which I had been raised. While there, God confirmed His leading. We were able to present our mission in person to Olivet Presbyterian, the church family where I had met Jesus. They, too, encouraged us, loved us, and sent us out with prayer and financial support. By the time we flew out of the United States we had raised *all* of our support needs for the field. "See if I will not throw open the floodgates of heaven and pour out so much blessing that you will not have room enough for it" (Malachi 3:10).

As we flew out of the country on Iceland Air, I reflected on what had happened to us in those few short months. I thought about how God had not chosen to bless us with a secure, prestigious job or with the financial status to buy a big, beautiful home and send our kids to great private schools. Instead, He chose to bless us abundantly and open up the floodgates of heaven so that His kingdom would be furthered and glorified through us in His power. That is a privilege beyond comprehension and a blessing I had not room enough for in my heart. He had blessed us far beyond what we deserved. It is an awesome feeling to know you are in the center of God's perfect will.

On May 8, 1986, Steven's fourth birthday, we flew over the waters of the Atlantic, eagerly looking toward the future. Our first stop was Switzerland, Helimission's headquarters, where we were to receive some orientation. Our next stop was just five days later in Douala, Cameroon, West Africa.

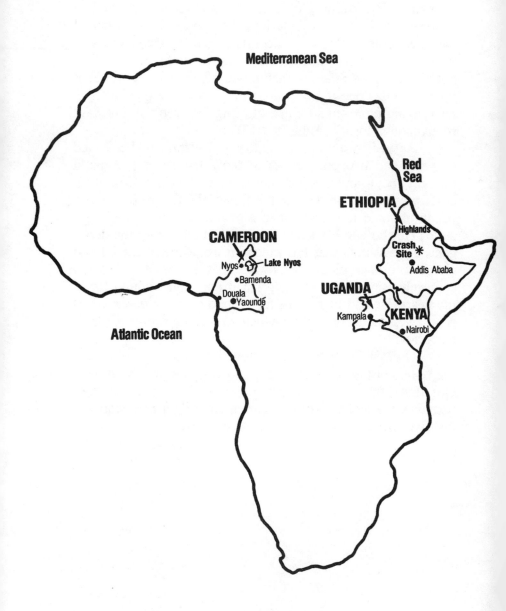

Mediterranean Sea

Red
Sea

ETHIOPIA

Highlands

CAMEROON

Crash
Site

Nyos • ⌒ — Lake Nyos

Addis Ababa

• Bamenda

UGANDA

Douala •
• Yaoundé

KENYA

Atlantic Ocean

Kampala •

• Nairobi

10
Africa

It was after dark when we arrived, so we headed to a small hotel for the night. As we drove through the bustling streets of Douala, Cameroon, our first impressions were "hot and sticky"—busy, crowded streets, crazy drivers, horns beeping, and taxis everywhere. Our room at the hotel had only two single beds, and we had to lay out mattresses on the floor for the boys. We sang songs of praise while we got ready for bed and thanked God for our safe arrival and for the new adventure before us.

The next morning we loaded up an old "combi" van and began a seven-hour ride through tropical countryside dotted with huts, marketplaces, villages, and people carrying loads of various sizes on their heads. The sun burned down with full intensity, and the air coming through the only two windows we could open in the van didn't help very much at all. We soon looked and felt as if we had been in the great jungles of Africa for weeks. The whole experience reminded me of something one might read about in a *National Geographic* magazine.

At the end of the long day we entered the city of Bamenda, high in the cool hills of the northwest province of Cameroon. We arrived at our new home at about 8:30 in the evening to find dinner prepared and waiting on the table. I had known I was going to have a national man to cook for me, but already I felt like someone out of "Lifestyles of the Rich and Famous." Maybe Africa wouldn't be so bad after all.

The following morning greeted us early, and it wasn't long before I discovered the hordes of insects with which I had to learn to live. In the first week alone we killed ants, silverfish, spiders, ticks, moths, daddy long-leggers, termites, and some squiggly little wormlike "guys." Usually, one or more of the things would join us for dinner or a bath, but we tried to keep the visits short. John, our cook and house steward, gave our floors a tick bath each week. Some insects we had never heard of before were unique to our area. I had three favorites: creechies, mango fly eggs, and jiggers.

Creechies are known as "blister bugs." They are long, skinny, and black—like maggots—with an orange ring around their bodies. If we got one on our skin, we had to blow it off quickly because brushing or plucking it off caused it to secrete a juice that produced a large blister. The longer distance we wiped to get it off, the longer the blister. The blisters were very painful and took a long time to heal.

Mango fly eggs were the most disgusting. The wind blew the eggs onto our clothes while they hung out to dry. If the egg touched us, it got under the skin and a small maggot began to grow. To remove the maggot, we first had to let it grow to maturity. When the bump looked like a pimple, we put Vaseline on it, which caused the little creature to squirm and pop out his ugly little head. Finally we had to squeeze him out, just like a pimple, being very careful not to sever it lest an infection develop on the site.

Jiggers were not as disgusting, but they were still nothing to deal with until after dinner. Jiggers are parasites that attach to the toes where the nail meets the skin. At first glance, they look like dead skin but then a black dot appears in the center of its circular shape. It continues to grow, and although not painful in the early stages, it literally eats you until you remove it. To do that, you must cut away the dead skin, squeeze the parasite out, then saturate the hole with alcohol or hydrogen peroxide.

Although we fought these creatures daily, they did not overwhelm us. In fact, we found ways to avoid them. The mango fly egg could be killed by ironing our clothes after drying them. We could keep the jigger away by wearing socks and shoes. The creechies were easy to notice and could be crushed with napkins. So, if God is calling you to the mission field, but you are deterred by a fear of insects, let me assure you that I hate bugs, too. Yet God is bigger than any insect you will ever encounter. He will give you the grace to overcome your fears, and the bugs will become a natural part of your existence. Don't let something as trivial as a bug keep you from obeying God's will for your life!

During our first week in Bamenda we explored our surroundings and got to know some of the other missionaries. We found that we actually lived in a "suburb" of the city called Nkwen (pronounced, "N-quin"). Our home was on a hill where four other missionaries and our national pastor, Pastor Njemo, lived. At the front base of the hill was a Bible college operated by the Full Gospel Mission, and the missionary couple overseeing the school lived across the dirt road with their three children. Directly below them was the Full Gospel Printing Press operated by the German missionaries who lived at the top of the hill.

Helimission's main house and hangar were located on the back side of the hill, which was where our mechanic Dean Yeoman lived with his wife, Kaylene, and their two children. Our home was down the road to the right about a tenth of a mile—just across from Pastor Njemo's. From our backyard we had a majestic view of two mountain ranges and, during the rainy seasons, four flowing waterfalls. Below us and toward the base of the nearest mountain was a swamp area, flourishing with tropical foliage and mosquitoes. In every direction huts, farmlands, and tin-roofed dwellings dotted the countryside, filling the outskirts of Bamenda with life and productivity.

The drive into the center of Bamenda took about ten minutes through streets lined with men, women, and children walking to their respective destinations. Taxis raced through the streets—sometimes stopping suddenly right in the middle of the road to let out their passengers. We were quickly forced to learn the rules for driving without rules. The main road through Bamenda was lined with shops, local craftsman, street merchants, and peddlers selling their wares. Finally came the main open marketplace. It was a large dirt lot covered with wooden stalls and plastic tarps in which vendors displayed their vegetables, fruits, meats, and staples. The national women were busy talking to each other and nursing their children, but the moment we walked by, they began to bargain and sell their wares, quick to let us know the price was "very good."

Steve particularly liked the meat stalls. The butcher would cut up a cow early in the morning and then display its head and feet so that customers could see its freshness. The meat slabs were laid out on a wooden block, with flies everywhere, and the buyer would point to the section of meat he wanted to buy. The butcher would wrap the meat in newspaper and give it to him. The operation was direct and simple—no packaged, refrigerated meat precisely weighed and computer priced. Steve took pictures to show the churches back home "the contrast of our everyday life to theirs."

Next to the open market, through an open doorway, were rows and rows of lean-tos cluttered with merchandise of every size, shape, and color—shoes, cassette tapes, cooking utensils, sewing notions, toys, beauty supplies, soaps, jewelry, luggage, radios, clocks, clothes, rugs, and stationery supplies, to name a few. We could have walked for hours and still not have seen it all. Once we found something we liked, bargaining was the only way to get it. I found great pleasure in bargaining with the nationals. It helped me to interact personally with the people—and the competition to always get their best price was challenging. My favorite phrase was "Nooo, i dear plenti!" (No, it's too expensive!) Yet I soon found that no matter how good a price I got from one vendor, another one claimed he would have sold the same item to me for even less. Bargaining was an art to the vendors, for their livelihood depended on their skill in keeping the price high and the buyer's interpretation of it low.

Steve and I took in everything. Cameroon created in us a new fascination for life and learning.

We had only been in Africa a week when Steve had his first "serious" missionary experience. It began routinely enough. The Helimission helicopter at our base had experienced a hard landing deep in the bush, damaging the turbine engine. Dean, the mechanic, needed to remove the damaged part and replace it with a rental engine until the old one could be repaired. Changing an engine in the bush took great skill and even greater patience, and Dean had already made several trips to the helicopter. He needed to make one more trip to complete the repairs and bring the helicopter back to Bamenda, where Steve and I would get to see it for the first time. Steve's job was to drive Dean five hours down a dirt road into the bush, drop him off, and return home. In the meantime Dean would hike another five hours to the helicopter itself, finish the repairs, and fly the helicopter back to the base.

During the jeep ride into the jungle Steve thought of earlier missionaries who had traveled on the very same road. *They didn't have it so bad!* It was fun to drive the four-wheel drive Russian jeep down the bumpy dirt roads. He was even beginning to think that he was in good enough shape to hike the additional five hours to the helicopter with Dean (who was quite fit and experienced) and was wishing that I had driven them into the bush so that he could have gone along.

Steve dropped Dean off at the river he had to cross before continuing his journey, then turned the jeep around and headed back. Twenty minutes into his return trip, the jeep got stuck in the mud. Try as he did, he could not budge it. Remembering that he had seen some villagers near a plow down the road, he headed optimistically in that direction. He soon came to the plow, but no one was there. He thought the villagers would soon return, so he sat down and waited. After two hours had gone by, the length of the usual afternoon break in Africa, he realized suddenly that it was Sunday, and no one would be returning to work that day.

Discouraged but not defeated, he set off for the next village. He walked two hours more in the heat of the African sun. Now keenly aware of an aching and tightening in his muscles, he was thankful he had not tried to make the five-hour hike with Dean.

He reached a creek and stopped to fill his water bottle and rest. As he bent down by the water's bank, he slipped on a rock and fell into the creek, dropping and breaking his bottle and cutting his finger on the glass. *What is God trying to show me?* he wondered as he pulled himself out of the water. It wasn't long before the evening rains came, and by the time he entered the village of Essu, he was tired, sore, wet, and hungry. He regretted his thoughts about the "ease" of the earlier missionary's life.

The villagers took him to a nearby Presbyterian church, where he met the national pastor, and the Lord supplied him with a hot meal and a nice place to spend the night. Steve had gone most of the day without eating and waited in anticipation for his dinner, but when the young girls served him meat with "pepe" on it, the meal burned like a fire in his mouth. One bite and—"Aaagh! Hot! Hot! Hot!" He quickly grabbed a bottle of fresh water, drinking from it until the sizzling began to cool. Catching his breath, he poured the soothing liquid down his tender throat until even the tingling warmth was doused and dissipating. Terribly embarrassed, he apologized to his host, who had been watching him with puzzled amusement. Some bread and bananas were brought to the table, which Steve ate ravenously. Within the hour he collapsed from exhaustion into a typical African bed made from a foam mattress.

Morning came quickly, but he was ready to face a new day. He took his first bush bath with a bucket of water and a small hose in the back of the compound, then, after breakfast,

94

found a bush taxi to bring him to Bamenda. By the time I saw him walking up the hill to the front gate of our home he looked totally exhausted. He told me about his ordeal in graphic detail while I fed him and stuck him into a tub of hot water. Only moments later, Dean flew the helicopter in for its grand homecoming, but Steve was in the tub, too sore to move. He had come to appreciate the pioneers, who didn't have helicopters or expensive jeeps to protect them from the rigors of the African jungle.

Steve's second African "experience" occurred during a trip back from Douala. We had both been losing weight as we adjusted to the new food, and even our hands and fingers had gotten thinner. One day Steve decided to stop and buy some sweet finger bananas to eat on his way home. After making his purchase, he drove along happily, peeling bananas and tossing the peels out the window. As he tossed his third banana peel, his wedding ring went right along with it. He pulled over quickly onto the dirt shoulder, where he saw a small ravine directly outside his window, and began a desperate search for the ring—but all he could find was a squashed and bruised banana peel.

With the helicopter in full operation, wc were soon busy helping to spread the good news of Christ. We were able to do that in many ways. We flew for a number of mission support programs and transported supplies and building materials for hospitals, orphanages, schools, and bush churches. We flew doctors and medical teams into remote areas to hold medical clinics for people whose only other medical resource was the local witch doctor. We flew for humanitarian organizations and special government programs. And the helicopter was always available in times of national disaster. It enabled us to express God's love in a practical way and gave credibility to our witness.

Steve and I loved going to the bush areas and meeting with the local people. Their life-style was so simple, their needs so great, and their appreciation so heartfelt, whatever we could do for them was worth the effort. As I thought of

America's technology and great wealth, I wondered, *What is it all for?* In these remote villages, a simple gesture of love has more meaning than anything a superpower, with all its resources, could offer. Even when we flew back to Bamenda, where the Western world had infiltrated the culture, smiles were harder to find, and business was the order of the day.

Living in Africa gave us the opportunity to bring some of the bush life home, and we adopted an assorted menagerie of pets. Upon our arrival in Cameroon we inherited a German shepherd named Springfield. This lovable creature, brought to Cameroon from the Netherlands, had but one flaw—he was tormented by ticks and flies. But since his job was to scare away the "tif-man" (thief-man), and since thieves were deathly afraid of big dogs, he was worth his weight in gold. We also had a cat named Caleb. He spent most of his days out in the fields hunting mice and occasionally catching one for us in the house. Caleb was Springfield's best friend, and we often found the cat sleeping on top of Springfield's stomach, taking in the afternoon sun. Isaac was an African gray parrot who thought himself the prince of pets. Steve was the only one who could get near him. He would place his finger right in front of Isaac's beak, and the bird would begin to "click." We finally decided that the parrot was trying to imitate the last sound in his name, "Isaac."

We continued to add to our pet family. One trip to Douala brought us into contact with a small monkey smuggled into the country by one of the sailors in port. The monkey had no home, and the manager of the small hotel we were staying in, knowing that we lived in the country, asked if we would be interested in the little guy. Steve was a pushover, and I watched in resignation as one furry creature (my husband) preened the other. Although the boys were a bit cautious about their excitable new friend, they were in happy agreement with Dad. Thus we added another "son," Maggie, to our family. I must admit he became a favorite companion and source of entertainment.

Last, but certainly not least, was a pet Steve in his "infinite wisdom" bought for five dollars at a roadside live meat market on the road from Douala. It resembled a cross between a hedgehog, an armadillo, and a porcupine, weighed about two pounds, and liked to curl up into a ball. We learned quickly that it was a night creature, burrowing frantically to get out of his box in the guest bathroom once it was dark. It turned out that "Joshua" was a bona fide anteater. It would be misleading to say that I was pleased when he joined us. What was I going to do with an anteater? How was I going to feed him? But Steve had an idea. That afternoon I found Joshua on a leash tied to the bottom of Maggie's cage in the back yard. Steve's thinking was that when Maggie dropped his food, the ants would come, and Joshua could eat to his heart's content. It sounded reasonable, but I must admit that it looked a little odd, if not silly, to have an anteater on a leash.

Days went by and everyone seemed to be adjusting well. Caleb would nap on Springfield, Maggie would swing and chatter in his cage while Joshua remained rolled up into a ball through the day, and Isaac kept a steady watch over his kingdom. One day, with all appearing normal, we left instructions with John, our cook, and took off for Douala on business. On the trip, we learned that our little Joshua was a special prize indeed. He was a pangolin, a rare form of anteater. Steve, an avid stamp collector, remembered buying a stamp of a pangolin and said he believed it was on the endangered species series. More than likely it was against the law for us even to keep him. We considered the possibility of letting him go, but if he were captured again, he might have been eaten as "bush meat"—so his chances of survival would have been even lower. As it turned out, events made the decision for us. When we returned home we found that Joshua had died during our absence. We were all very sad, for we had learned too late of the value of our fragile friend.

Just a few days later, a terrible brush fire threatened to wipe out our ministry. Such fires were a daily occurrence during the "harmattan," or dry season, and most missionaries were aware of them and knew how to fight them. This particular fire came swiftly. It held great danger for us because a huge field full of tall, dry grass separated the two Helimission houses. Both houses had an area outside their fences where the grass was cut low as a safeguard against fire, but the height of the flames from the field between the two houses could have reached our homes quite easily.

The hangar full of fuel drums and the fueled helicopter sitting on the tarmac ready for its next mission served to heighten the danger of the situation. The men fought the fire bravely—fortunately their only injuries were minor scorching of the skin and singed hair on the arms—and God was merciful and faithful. The fire came up to both our fences but did not reach our homes. Two houses under construction on the compound had piles of wood stacked around them, but they too were left untouched—as if the fire had simply gone around them. Trees in our backyards that stood in the path of the fire remained unharmed. Ashes completely filled our houses, but nothing was burned.

We praised God for His watchful eye over our ministry, and once again we were reminded of the importance of the helicopter in the overall mission of spreading the gospel of Jesus Christ. A ministry that is fruitful is always attacked by the enemy, but God rules over the circumstances for the purpose of His glory. It was for His glory that we were protected in that situation.

Life in Africa was far from dull, no doubt about it, and there were joys in even routine activities. One day we brought Steven and Colby with us on a flight to the bush village of Adere to pick up a mission nurse involved in an immunization program. When we reached the village the boys quickly became the center of attention. All afternoon a crowd of children chased them and played with them. Steven would run through the crowd like a defensive tackle trying to sack the quarterback. The children loved it. They picked him up and carried him like the coach of the winning team. He was king of the day, and he enjoyed every minute of it! Colby was a little more intimidated by the crowds, but at one point we were able to get him to flex his muscles, to the delight of the children.

Everywhere we went that day we had an audience. Villagers even peered into the window of our mud hut so that Steve couldn't change his clothes in privacy. Still, we had a pleasant evening, and over a meal of millet cakes and chicken cooked in palm oil we learned about the success of the immunization program. The shots had been given in the village church, and before the medical clinic began, the gospel of Christ was shared. Many of the villagers came to know the Lord, and although the benches, made with round logs and set on stone, were not comfortable to sit on, the praises the people lifted up to God were as beautiful as those in any church or fancy cathedral throughout the world. We left the village tired and in desperate need of a bath but were again exhilarated and humbled by the fact that God had allowed us to share in the lives of the people of Adere and to glimpse what He was doing in their hearts.

11
Mysterious Disaster

During the third week of August 1986, an itinerant Baptist minister went into a village called Nyos in the upper northwest province, an area heavily populated by the Funlani tribe, who were wandering Muslim herdsmen and warriors. While there, the minister presented the gospel of Jesus Christ. He left Thursday afternoon, knowing that fifteen of the eight hundred villagers had made sincere commitments to accept Jesus as their Lord and Savior.

That evening at about 9.00 P.M. a volcanic lake just above the village mysteriously emitted a lethal gas, which traveled down into the valley and through the little town. Most of the people were asleep in their beds, but some were by their cooking fires, and some were talking among themselves in small groups. Without warning and within minutes, the village of Nyos was quietly decimated by the unseen force—the victims unaware that an enemy had come.

The gas crept silently to surrounding areas, where more unsuspecting villagers met their deaths. As the gas seeped into still other regions, it became more selective. Two men stood together talking—one died and the other survived. As a family slept together in a hut, five died, and two were left.

"Therefore keep watch, because you do not know on what day your Lord will come. . . . So you also must be ready, because the Son of Man will come at an hour when you do not expect him." (Matthew 24:42, 44).

For the people of Nyos, the hour came quickly; but God in His mercy had provided a way of escape. Fifteen people had chosen that way. Fifteen people were found "faithful and sensible," ready for the arrival of their Lord. Approximately eight hundred others from the village of Nyos were not.

News of the disaster spread quickly south toward the more populated regions, but the villagers and government officials who were posted in the bush areas were fearful of going to the affected area, thinking that they too might die. It wasn't until Saturday, when Dean was flying a Baptist doctor up to the border that he first heard about it. Bad weather had forced Dean to land in Essu, and one of the village men asked him if he had heard about the deaths up by the lake. Dean told him he hadn't. So when the weather cleared, the medical team was taken up to the border for the day, and before Dean returned to Bamenda, he diverted east to the village of Nyos. As he approached the area, he was amazed by what he found. What had once been a beautiful dark blue lake with a majestic waterfall was now crude brown with black and rust-colored streaks running through it. There was debris on the water everywhere. The water level itself was down about four feet and the waterfall was dry. There was evidence of a massive washout on the opposite side of the lake.

As he flew closer, he could see dead cattle strewn all over the hillside. In the village he saw bodies throughout most of the compounds, but a few people were moving about, so he decided to land. A Catholic priest was there, and together they went into the various compounds searching for survivors. What they found was horrible, tragic death everywhere.

The silence was so complete it could be felt; not even the sound of insects could be heard. Nyos was like a ghost-town in the American West, eerily reminiscent of a once thriving community but stripped of life. Most people had died in their beds. Whole families were found together. Some looked as though they had tried to make it to their doorways. Some had made it as far as the yard within their compound structure. There were dead goats, dogs, cats, chickens, birds, and even frogs scattered every place Dean went.

Only six persons had survived. They were gathered in the marketplace at the center of the village. Dean asked them what had happened, but only one lady could answer: "I felt the earth bump and fell into my cooking fire." She was severely burned on her right arm, and she was evacuated immediately by helicopter to a nearby hospital along with three others who were seriously ill. The remaining two seemed to be fine and suffered no ill effects, but they also were flown out for observation.

The following day, Steve and Dean returned to the area, bringing fresh water and supplies. Outside relatives of the Nyos victims had started to trickle in to dig the mass graves. One man from Bamenda, a postal headmaster at the Nkwen office, buried fifty-six members of his family that day. Both Steve and Dean did what they could to comfort the people by joining in to help.

By Monday word of the disaster had reached the international press, and within twenty-four hours the Western world was bombarding us. Reporters heard about our helicopter housed only twenty minutes from the disaster area and hastily made their way to Bamenda. For documentation purposes Dean had taken many excellent pictures of the disaster the first day he was in the village. He took those pictures at some risk because the government had a strict policy about photographs. Immediately, the pictures were made known to government officials in Bamenda, and they called Steve and Dean down for a meeting. It was agreed that one set of the pictures would be sent to the Cameroonian government and one set would be retained by Helimission, for the government believed that we were not there to exploit the people.

The next day Dean and Steve were out flying, Dean's wife, Kaylene, was working the radio for flight following, and I was helping with the influx of the media. A reporter for an American weekly newsmagazine showed up at our home and

103

began to question me about flying up to the area and buying our set of pictures. The reporter badgered me about the pictures, and taking into consideration that I lived there as a missionary, he said, "God would want the world to know the truth, and since I can give them the truth, don't you think God would want me to have those pictures?"

Seeing that I remained unimpressed he continued, "How about letting me just take pictures of your pictures? No one will ever know!"

Then he attempted to reach me through my "piety." "I see that you care about these people a great deal, and I just want the world to see how they can help. I promise, it will be worth it to you."

Finally I told him, "You know, in a week or so you will be gone from here, working on another story, not caring in the least about these people, their plight, or their dead. However, we will still be living here and working among them on a daily basis. Not only are we representatives of our respective countries, but we are representatives of God. This government has already shown us that they trust us by allowing us to keep the film. They believe we will not exploit their people in any way—and that includes giving photographs to you just so you can have dead people on your magazine cover rather than dead cows. As for your claim that 'No one will ever know,' well, God will certainly know, and it is because of Him most of all that I cannot give them to you."

As it turned out, not one gory picture was released for better T.V. or magazine ratings even though the price offered had reached into the thousands.

Relief efforts were soon in full operation. Governments from all over the world assisted by sending supplies, financial aid, and relief teams. Refugee camps were established, doctors and humanitarian groups were flown in to help, and scientists were taken to the disaster scene to find out what had caused the volcanic lake to suddenly erupt with such lethal effects. About a month after the disaster, news began to filter in that some of the victims had left their villages to travel to remote areas where they had extended families. Those victims had left before receiving medical treatment, and we knew they were suffering from burns, breathing problems, and other ill effects of the gas. The General Baptist Conference wanted to send out a medical team, so Steve and I flew up to one of their bush hospitals to pick up a doctor. Then we flew into the remote villages, where we found victims whose burns were scarred over and deeply infected. We spent the day assisting the doctor, giving out medications, and cleaning burns. To me, it was a practical way to show the people that we cared for them and that they were not forgotten. *This*, I thought, *was one of the reasons I wanted to come to Africa.* God truly had been faithful: He had given me a love for the people that was real and from my heart. We left that day knowing we had accomplished something for the kingdom.

The weather on the return trip was terrible, and rain clouds closed in on us rapidly. Visibility was extremely low, and many times we had to divert from our flight path to avoid storms and clouds. Steve's flying skills were stretched to the limit as we flew barely above the treetops on our way to Bamenda. The Lord was with us every step of the way. But the devil was not going to take such a day of victory sitting down.

Each evening the helicopter had to be rolled into the hangar. To do this, a devise called a ground-handling wheel was placed under each landing skid. These wheels allowed the helicopter to be pushed easily in and out of the hangar. As Steve and Dean were attempting to put the helicopter to bed, the metal bar Steve was using to lock the ground-handling wheel onto the skid of the helicopter flew up from its tensed position, hit him on the lower jaw, and sent him flying through the air. He landed five feet away, near the tail rotor.

I was at home when I got the call, and when I saw him, he was lying on the ground in Dean's lap with a puzzled look on his face. He had a ragged cut on his lower right jaw and was apparently suffering from a concussion. He kept asking, "What happened?" But when we explained it to him, he repeated, "Yeah . . . but what happened?" That went on for a few minutes until I took him back in time to a point where he did remember something.

"Do you remember working at the typewriter?" I asked.

"Yes." He replied.

"Do you remember feeding the dog?"

"Yes."

"Do you remember telling me that you were going to go back down to the hangar to put the helicopter away?"

"Yes."

"Do you remember kissing your bee-uu-tiful wife good-bye?" I teased.

"No?" he queried in his most dramatic and least convincing stupor, the twinkle in his eye only too obvious. I knew then that he was still with us and that he would be OK.

We lugged him into the van and took him to the hospital, where he received four or five stitches. By morning he appeared to have recovered and was even bragging enthusiastically about his first set of stitches in his thirty-five years of life. If I had had a lollipop, I'd have given it to him.

A couple of weeks later, at the end of September, Dean and Kaylene left for Switzerland for two months of language school and a well-deserved furlough. Our prayer request to our supporters back home was that nothing would go wrong with the helicopter while Dean was gone, since he was the mechanic. But unfortunately, the ground-handling wheel, which we had affectionately nicknamed "Killer Wheel," continued to cause us problems. The day after Dean and Kaylene left, the tire blew up while Steve was putting a little air into it. The problem before us was how to get the helicopter out of the hangar with only one wheel for two skids. Five men and ten skid rotations later, we finally got it to its take-off position. For about two days we had no further problems, but early one morning the helicopter wouldn't start. Steve did everything he possibly could and even called mechanics as far away as France. We soon realized that it was not a routine problem.

We were both frustrated and depressed, so while Steve continued working at the hangar, I went home and agonized in my prayer journal. I even begged God to give us wisdom to understand the problem with the helicopter.

O Lord, there seem to be trials for Helimission every day. Satan longs to frustrate our efforts here. People will begin to think that they cannot depend on us. O God, have mercy. Dean is gone. There is no mechanic here! The helicopter won't start. O Lord, in your infinite wisdom, give Steve the understanding to know what the problem may be. Father, allow Your work to continue without delay and without these constant interruptions. It is for Your glory that the helicopter is here. Please use it for Your glory! Dash to pieces the efforts of the enemy to halt us. O Lord, give us grace to see this problem to victory. Let Your victory be soon. Do not make the enemy's attacks more than we can bear. Make a way of escape!

Reveal Your hand in Helimission. We need You so much to keep us operating. Do not hide Your face from us. Forgive us for our sin and our inadequacies in serving You. Help us to spread the gospel. Help us to be a light in this wilderness. I have no pride because I know I need You to be a success in anything. Please, oh please, Lord, let my interceding be enough. Let my prayer touch Your heart to action. Let the burden of my heart not escape the mercy of Your power. Help us, Lord. It's time to push forward the work You have called us to do! No more delays! No more heartache! But the triumph of your gospel! O God, You alone.

Some people might not resort to such begging, but I can't begin to describe how good Jesus is. Steve went to Douala the following morning to pick up a helicopter part the mechanics in France thought might solve the problem. While he was there, he went to a helicopter company that worked off the coast with some oil rigs. They had a mechanic—an electrical engineer, to be exact—and the company said we could borrow him. Steve brought him back to Bamenda, and although he didn't speak a bit of English, he worked diligently with an interpreter and our manual—and found the source of the problem! It was a "worn relay" in the electrical panel of the starting cycle. The miracle was that that mechanic was spending his last week in Cameroon before going back to France. His company was not going to replace him with another electrical engineer. My question was, *Why didn't the relay "wear" just one more week?* Answer: *Because God is faithful.* It was a test for us to trust His all-knowing power and to see a revelation of His love when we were without our mechanic. It was again a reassurance of Helimission's call to serve Jesus in Cameroon.

The engineer hot-wired the helicopter until we could get a new relay from Europe. In the meantime, we were scheduled to take the *National Geographic* Science Team up to Lake Nyos for further studies of the disaster. We strapped ourselves in, and Steve began the checklist for starting the helicopter. The starting cycle began winding up and the rotor blades began to turn slowly—when, suddenly, they slowed to a small whir, and the hum of the engines died. We had blown a fuse because of the hot-wiring.

We tried two more fuses, and twice more they blew. I picked up the next to last fuse, and before handing it to Steve I prayed aloud, "O Lord, please anoint this fuse." I passed the fuse to Steve, and he carefully snapped it into place. He pushed the starter button on the rotor lever, and a steady building power surged through the helicopter. The glass on the fuse broke, and the wire inside bent, but the helicopter started. The sound was music from heaven. That same little fuse started the helicopter more than forty times before the replacement part finally arrived from Europe.

Does God answer prayer? Wow! What a demonstration of His power in our lives! What a witness to the *National Geographic* team. I have no idea what they thought of it, but I do know that they heard that prayer and were just as happy as we were about its results! God showed us again that His work is not dependent upon a mechanic but upon His grace and Spirit. We took our eyes off our own limitations and trusted God for the time Dean would be gone.

August 30, 1980, at Olivet Presbyterian Church.
Visions of living "happily ever after."

Musicians playing the chong (top); ju-jus (witch doctors) dancing (middle and lower pictures).

An African church.

Maggie helps me write letters home.

Christina Joan at the peak of her health
two weeks before her death.

Colby helps his dad with
repairs (top); Steven in his
dining room "school"
(middle); Steven and
Colby in our backyard in
Cameroon (lower).

Steve and I and Colby and Steven in the helicopter (left);
Christmas in Cameroon (right).

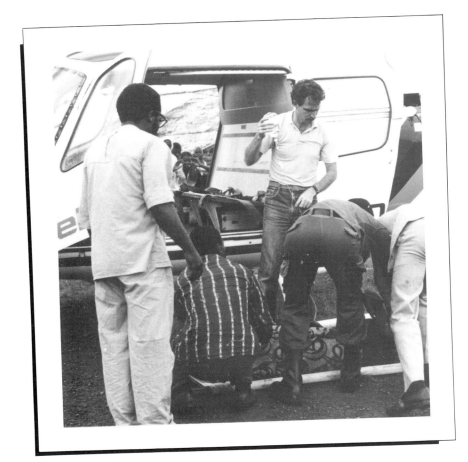

Steve assisting as medical personnel
prepare a person for evacuation.

Medical evacuation to the Helimission helicopter.

Colby Matthew's casket (left) and burial marker (right).

Steve and I with my mother and Steven
after Colby Matthew's death.

The crash site, ten minutes by air from Addis Ababa, Ethiopia.

Lowering Steve's casket into the ground (upper left);
the gravesite service (lower left);
gravestones for Steve and Troy (right).

Our last family portrait.

12
The Cry-Die

In November 1986, three months after the Nyos disaster, we heard that there was going to be a "cry-die," or wake, on behalf of those who had died there. By that time most of the survivors had resettled or moved to refugee camps. Steve and I wanted to go to show our respect for the dead as well as see the ritual of mourning, which would help us better understand the people and the spiritual implications of death for them.

The cry-die was hosted by a large Catholic diocese. We watched as the mass was performed by the national priests and hundreds of people came forward to receive the "bread of life." When the service ended, Steve and I were invited to share in a great feast of all the local dishes. We learned from talking with some of the sisters that more than eight thousand people were at the cry-die, representing villages all over the northwest province. The sisters told us that after the meal many of the villages would be represented in dance as they paraded in respect for the dead before the surviving chief of Nyos. Both Steve and I were shocked to hear that the ceremonial rites would be held on the very same ground as the mass of Jesus. Yet we later learned that even an Islamic service had been held earlier that morning on the same site.

We finished our meal and began making our way back to the festivities when Curt Stager, from *National Geographic*, came and told us that his team had been granted permission to interview the chief of Nyos. Quickly we asked if we could be present, and after asking the proper officials we were invited to attend. The audience was held in a small hut, and many other chiefs of the surrounding villages were present as well. All the women who had been serving the meal were sent out, and, as the only woman present, I was seated near the wall and asked to keep quiet.

The chief was asked various questions concerning the loss of his tribe. Through the young national serving as his interpreter, he told us how saddened he was by the tragedy. He explained that he had been out of the village that day because of business with another chief. He had taken one of his young daughters with him, and now they were facing the crisis of mourning and finding a place to resettle. He allowed us to take a few pictures before we left. The lack of hope in his eyes was striking.

The personal devastation for the chief was heightened by his belief in ancestors. The lakes are objects of worship because the people believe that chiefs (also called "fons") and other important men of the tribes live in the lakes after they die. The people seldom washed clothes or bathed in the lakes because many believed that a "Mammy Water" spirit resided in them. The spirit was thought to lure unsuspecting swimmers or fishermen to tragic and untimely deaths. In that culture, where spirits and dead ancestors are a part of everyday life, a disaster such as the one at Nyos was understood as a curse. Even apart from the disaster, the people often offered animal and food sacrifices to the lakes and rivers to appease the spirits, in the hope that the spirits would live at peace with the people. The people believed that if the spirits were kept happy, the rains would come, the crops flourish, and disasters not occur. So to have an entire village wiped out could only mean that all their ancestors (their gods) had been angered beyond the appeasement of any sacrifice.

Africans fear their dead and show respect for them, usually by burying them inside their huts or somewhere within their compound structure. They believe that each time they pass over the grave they receive some of that ancestor's wisdom or good qualities. If the dead person was considered bad or evil, they bury him in the woods. Steve and I were careful to keep all these beliefs in mind as we settled on a place to sit and watch the ceremonies.

The ju-jus (witch doctors) were adorned in colorful attire with feathers and wood-carved masks depicting various animals or significant ancestors. The masks were not just decoration—the ju-jus believe they become the actual spirit of the mask they wear. The masks were large, black, and heavy. Some fit over the dancer's face, but some were worn on top of the head, with the face of the mask pointed skyward. Some ju-jus wore heavy bracelets made from kola nuts around their ankles and covered their faces with burlap sacks. The sacks had straw and dry grass woven in on top for hair. Children ju-jus also lined up on one side of the grounds. For many of them it was their first public demonstration of the already deeply rooted beliefs of their ancestors.

Although there were many traditional musicians with drums, cows' horns, and seed shakers, to my amusement the first set of dancers filed in to Jamaican reggae music blaring loudly from expensive ghetto blasters bought in the cities. The women wore wrap-around skirts with only a bra on their upper bodies. They remained bent at the waist while they danced, so as to show respect for the meaning of the dance, we later learned. One of the most interesting groups of women dancers was the one that played the "chong," a calabash (gourd) with the neck broken off. The dancers blew through a sugar cane reed like a tuba while projecting up and down inside the calabash. The chongs were painted bright red and gave out rich baritone sounds.

The dances went on for quite some time, each village bringing its individual cultural flavor. The ju-ju dancers were by far the most powerful and electrifying for the crowds. They

111

danced feverishly, and I could feel the earth shake as their bare feet pounded on the ground directly in front of me. They shouted and screamed and rushed into the crowds, scaring them with their sticks and magical powers. The gendarmes present to keep order whipped the legs of the observers to keep them from grabbing the ju-ju dancers. Panic broke out in small patches, and children were almost trampled as the mob swelled closer and farther from the reach of the whips.

Finally, the last villages finished their dances. With whistles blowing, palm leaves and tree branches waving in the air, and countless ghetto blasters screaming different songs, the mob of dancers moved in for one last celebration as the crowd of onlookers began to disperse. The mood was ominous in its energy. Steve and I were pressed against the chairs where the traditional chiefs had been sitting. We began to push through the crowds and confusion, losing each other in the fight. Only when we were near our jeep did we spot one another again.

Paul says in Ephesians, "Our struggle is not against flesh and blood, but against the rulers, against the authorities, against the powers of this dark world and against the spiritual forces of evil in the heavenly realms" (Ephesians 6:12). The people in the crowd that day did not need to be told they were fighting a spiritual battle, that they were not fighting against flesh and blood. But without the knowledge of Jesus Christ they fell into the same trap as other pagan religions—attempting by good works and sacrifice to please God and win blessings and favor—and thereby missed the salvation that comes through the atoning sacrifice of Christ.

Many people view Africa as a dark and spiritually foreboding country, a place where satanic spiritism runs rampant. But in actuality it is a country of people looking for answers. Who brings the rains? Who causes the sun to set and the moon to shine in the dark night sky? Where do the spirits of the dead go? What makes the spirit of a man good or evil? How do we get along with the rulers of the earth? Without the gospel of Christ, the people find their answers in the ju-ju. To them, he holds the powers and secrets of the spirit world and rules the people with fear. They must obey him by sacrificing their animals, giving abundant gifts, and honoring the spirits of their ancestors. Yet in spite of all that, they have no hope and no eternal purpose for their lives.

The gospel provides the true answers to the questions the Africans ask. God loves the people of Africa. Jesus died for their sin, and God offers them a new life—a life without the fear of evil. He offers a life that acknowledges that our battle is with Satan and that acknowledges as well that our victory is in Jesus, the Son of God, who shed His innocent blood on a cross to equip us triumphantly for the struggle against the rulers, authorities, and powers of this dark world, the spiritual forces of evil. The battle is not for good rains or a plentiful crop but for the soul.

Many times humanitarian workers accuse missionaries of trying to rob the Africans of their distinctive culture. The Africans have survived for centuries in peace believing their own religions, they say. Why do you have to change their God? The answer is simple: because there is no salvation apart from Christ. "Whoever believes in the Son has eternal life, but whoever rejects the Son will not see life, for God's wrath remains on him" (John 3:36).

Paul says in Romans 1:14 that we are obligated to the wise and to the foolish. We are obligated to cultures of high technology as well as to those living simply and close to the land. If I truly believe that Jesus is the only answer and that in Jesus alone there is a hope for the men and women of this world, how can I not be obligated? Paul goes on to say, "How, then, can they call on the one they have not believed in? And how can they believe in the one of whom they have not heard? And how can they hear without someone preaching to them? And how can they preach unless they are sent? As it is written, 'How beautiful are the feet of those who bring good news!' " (Romans 10:14-15) The missionary goes because he *must* go.

We saw the victory of the gospel of Jesus Christ in Cameroon. Although is it very hard for the African Christian to put behind him cultural beliefs that are opposed to the gospel, God is doing a marvelous work among them, and the zeal of the Lord is evident. They have a hope and a message to share with their fellow tribesmen because the African, once shown the light and true meaning of the gospel, understands more clearly than we ever could the depth of the bondage that chains his people. African believers have a much greater burden to bring about a change in their own people's hearts than we can understand, because they were once there themselves.

That truth was emphasized more clearly for me when we flew sixty-five Bible students from a Baptist college in Ndu to thirty-four villages surrounding the disaster area of Lake Nyos. From those villages, the students trekked farther to even more remote areas. They stayed one week to share the gospel, and in that area where three months earlier only 15 people had made sincere commitments to the Lord, in one week more than 1,340 people chose to make Jesus their personal Lord.

The people were reaching for an answer, and what Satan had intended for destruction, God turned into glory. If not for the lake disaster, the individuals in that heavily Muslim and traditionally tribal cult area would not have been open to their need for a God who had a greater power and meaning than the objects and ancestral spirits they were currently worshiping.

What touched me most profoundly was what happened in the months following. When the students came back from the disaster area they told us that the Christians living there were very discouraged and felt that the disaster had been a judgment of God upon them. In their deep concern and love for these believers, the students decided to go back to the region on their Christmas break for the sole purpose of encouraging and edifying the hurting Body of Christ. They desired to restore the faith of their brothers and sisters in a personal God who loved them. I wondered, *How many of us would give up our holidays—our time with our families, all our gifts, and all the festivities—to encourage people we hardly knew simply because they were discouraged?*

We had experienced so much in such a short time that it was hard to believe Christmas was already upon us. But in Cameroon even Christmas became a new experience. We learned how beautiful the celebration of Christ's birth can be without the commercial tinsel and bright lights. While Daddy was busy flying, the boys and I made a colorful paper chain to decorate the walls and the small tree we had borrowed from some friends. I found an old sock and some yarn and made a singing angel for the top of the tree, and we further adorned it with hard-baked flour decorations.

Steve and I sneaked out the afternoon before Christmas while the boys were taking their naps and went to the main market. We were joyfully surprised to see the streets filled with people. Taxis could barely squeeze through as vendors lined the roads with carts and boxes full of merchandise. Bells were ringing, whistles were blowing, ghetto blasters were filling the air with Christmas music, and vendors were shouting persuasive arguments to potential customers. One of their favorite attention-getters when I walked by was, "Hey, Mrs. Reagan! Buy from me!" The crowds were exhilarated, and there were greetings and handshakes all around.

The following morning the boys awoke to two brand new bicycles, a couple of toys, and some candy. Our tree didn't overflow with gifts, but we could certainly see the joy of the celebration on Steven and Colby's faces as they raced their new bikes around the living room. Later that morning we attended a small service at our church and shared the celebration of the birth of Christ, singing carols with a few of our national friends. Mid-afternoon we went to the hangar where missionaries of every denomination gathered to celebrate with a barbecue. The men carried my electric piano outside, Dean played the saxophone, and another friend, Jonathan, brought his guitar. As we played, everyone joined in to sing the carols of the season, helping us to feel as if we were "home." It was a Christmas laced with simplicity—and was one of the most enjoyable Christmases we had ever had.

Africa. It seemed like the perfect life-style for all of us. Every day was filled with a new experience, whether it was hauling buckets for a bath, bargaining at the market, feeding our pet monkey, or watching a video with the other missionaries. We knew we were privileged to be there, and our hearts were free to love Jesus no matter what the circumstances around us. Yet, even in Africa God does not stop His children's growth, and the next few months brought God's love closer to my heart than it had ever been before.

13
Parting

In early January our director sent a telex from Switzerland asking Steve to go to Uganda to help set up a new Helimission station there. The request sounded wonderful for the mission, and it was a great opportunity for Steve, but my heart sank. He would be gone for at least two months, and neither my mind nor my heart was prepared for another separation.

I'm sure that much of my disappointment stemmed from selfishness. I loved being in the middle of ministry with Steve, and now he would be going into a new adventure without me. God had to work on my heart.

That evening I listed in my prayer book the blessings of ministry I already had. I counted the two most important as being a mom and teaching Steven school each day. I tried to rest in those blessings, but the pain of letting Steve go ran deep. As the day of his departure neared, tensions between us grew. After many weeks of the strain, I wrote a dear friend two letters about my feelings:

Dear Deanna,   1-16-87

Just a quick note to say I love you, and hope all is going well. Not all is going well here. With Steve leaving for Uganda on Feb. 6th, things are tense. I thought I left these

117

separations behind when we left the military, but alas. (Heavy sigh!) To be honest, he's not helping matters. When he's in a good mood, I'm supposed to be in a good mood; when he wants to be left to sulk, I'm to shut up. I guess it's one of those times when no matter what you do, it's not enough. It happens before every long separation—to make the departure less painful you insult and hurt each other to convince yourselves you need the separation, and it will be good for both of you. A prime example of satanic attack. Please pray for me, I don't think I'm handling it very well.

Love,
Kathy

Hi Deanna! 2-5-87

Well, Steve leaves me for Uganda tomorrow. So how do I feel about all this? (Heavy sigh again!) Mixed feelings, of course. Feeling pretty lousy one minute, okay the next, and always realizing God's power and love is greater than my feelings. Regardless, His joy shall be the countenance on my face!

Many times in the military I sent my husband off for long periods of time, yet now in the name of Jesus he goes to a country more unstable than any he went to as a marine. Strange, huh? Of course I can't help wondering what will happen, and although I can't let my imagination run away from me, I know Christians are not exempt from the cruelties of this world. Being in aviation, we must be candid when we speak about life and death. So as much as I try to avoid "the talk," at least I have the comfort of being somewhat prepared, not only spiritually and emotionally, but financially.

This may seem silly to most people, but even separations are a sort of death, and if I can't face that, how will I face the real thing? As difficult as this is, I will always understand this one truth:

118

God is on the throne.
Jesus is at His right hand in all
power and glory, and the
Holy Spirit works a mighty deed
throughout the earth in the
hearts of men!

As in all things, it comes down to one thing . . . no, one person: Jesus. And He loves me. He is the strength of my life.

Okay, enough of that. I feel better and lifted up already. Isn't God wonderful? How do people live without Him? It's truly amazing, isn't it?

I love you, Deanna. Thank you for being there for me.

Love,
Kathy

On the morning of February 6, Steve was ready to go. Dean and Kaylene and our family went to Douala in the combi van to take Steve to the airport. Steve sensed the turmoil in my heart and was very understanding. Most of the trip he let me rest my head in his lap and entertained the boys with toys and books. I didn't feel any pressure to join the conversation with forced joy or congeniality. Before Steve boarded the airplane he said, "I'm hoping that you get a chance to come over and visit with me while I'm there. I'll talk to Ernie and see what I can do."

When I got back to Bamenda, my emotions were so bottled up I thought I would explode, so I wrote a song to the Lord.

Take My Heart, Sweet Jesus

What is this inside me?
The hurt I can't express?
Why does it surround me?

119

I can't get any rest.
I need to cry out to You,
I need to let it go,
I need to give it to You,
I need to let it show.

What is this I long for?
The fullness of Your love.
To fill the void inside me,
the pain that stabs my heart.
I need to pour out to You,
To see Your love is there.
I need to surrender,
Every part of me to Your care.

So take my heart, sweet Jesus.
Take it and make it Yours.
Mold me into Your likeness,
In this I'll be secure.
Jesus . . . Jesus . . . how my spirit cries.

Two weeks later we heard from Steve. He sent a telex informing us he had heard that the helicopter stationed at our Ethiopian base had crashed, that there had been no injuries, and—almost as an afterthought—that he had been arrested in Uganda. He left a number where I could reach him, but as was typical, it was impossible to get through on the African phone system. After many unsuccessful attempts, all I could do was trust Jesus that he was all right.

In the meantime, I was asked to teach English at the Full Gospel Bible College in place of the director's wife, Judy Treherne, who had become ill. Judy told me that just being able to speak English qualified me for the job and that the books would tell me what to do. Although it was entirely new to me, teaching the students became a great source of joy. As an incentive for the class, I introduced ten new words to them every week and asked them to put each word into sentence form after we had discussed its meaning.

One day I had an especially difficult time with the lesson as I attempted to explain the word *hockey* to the students. I went into great detail about the sport and even tried to draw a hockey puck and stick on the board. But confusion still filled their faces. Then I realized it was not the hockey puck and stick that caused their confusion. They were wondering about the "floors of ice" and the "shoes with thin metal bars"!

Two weeks later I heard from my mother, who got her mail from Steve faster than I did, and she told me that he had been arrested while doing a training flight for the new Helimission pilot. Steve had obtained what he thought were all the proper flight permissions from the military, the government, and the airport; but too many people in Third World nations have rubber stamps, and each person thinks his is the most important. The military police of the National Resistance Alliance had ordered Steve and the new pilot to land and had held them for questioning. After a good deal of browbeating and threats, including a charge of spying, they were released.

The result of the meeting was that although Helimission had been invited to Uganda by Christians within the government structure, the politically unstable country was too dangerous for a mission such as ours to operate safely there. The chances of getting shot down were too great, even though the helicopter did have a big red cross on its belly.

Back in Bamenda, while waiting to hear further from Steve, I entertained a house guest for a month. Her name was Carol, and she had come to our northwest province to teach the people in the bush churches how to hold a Sunday school. On the weekends she went to the bush villages to teach seminars and then returned for the week to rest, replenish her personal chocolate supply, and prepare for the next weekend.

My children loved their "Aunty Miss Carol"—and especially her skills as a ventriloquist. Her monkey puppet-friend, Natasha, would visit Steven and Colby at least once a day. The real treat was watching John, our cook, stare at that puppet. He could not figure out how Natasha could talk without a tongue. He would stare and stare. Once, he asked if that kind of monkey was found only in the United States.

Some of the nationals believed that Natasha was magic, some believed that Carol used a tape recorder, and still others thought Natasha was real. Carol had to explain how she controlled Natasha (and gave away trade secrets in the process), so that the nationals didn't think she used ju-ju powers.

We had many good times with Aunty Miss Carol. The most memorable was the time we took Colby, who was almost three and a half, to a bush hospital to have a circumcision performed by an American doctor. Everything went quite smoothly at the hospital except for one moment of fear. The doctor asked me to hold Colby while he received a shot in his thigh. Colby squeezed his arms tightly around my neck and cried as the medicine went in, but within a few minutes he began to get drowsy. All of sudden his body went limp, and as the nurse lifted him out of my arms, the faraway look in his eyes shot my memory to visions of Christina. A shudder of panic pierced my heart. Immediately I sent up a prayer to God and went looking for Carol, who had taken Steven for a walk. Feeling the warmth of the morning sun as I walked through the hospital courtyards helped to wash away the coldness of that terrible vision.

A half hour later, Colby emerged from the operating room with no complications. When he recognized me he said, "No more shots?" I said, "No, honey, no more shots." He smiled and replied, "I want Fanta," and then slipped back into a deep sleep. My heart was overwhelmed with love for my little trooper, and Carol and I laughed as she agreed to go into town to buy Colby a Fanta orange drink.

That evening we stayed in a small bush motel, and after our star patient checked out of the hospital the following morning, we headed back to Bamenda on the dusty dirt roads. Little did we know that we were in for our first and only "African safari."

When we first noticed our prey, we quickly pulled over to the side of the dirt road. With lightening speed we evacuat-

122

ed the car and raced to get our weapon from the trunk. Once we were properly positioned, we aimed and fired. But our prey was only wounded and limped off to find a hiding place. I looked at Carol and asked, "Do you think we will see him again?"

"I don't know," she replied.

"There he is! Kill him! Get him now!" I shouted.

Another aim—and fire!

"Did we get him? I think we got him. Yes, he's mortally wounded. His feet are up in the air. They're still kicking, but just barely," I cried with a sigh of relief.

As we walked over to assess the kill, we both agreed that he was finally dead. We did it! In a unanimous decision we decided not to take him back for mounting. We left him in the dust under the hot African sun, and put our can of RAID back into the trunk. We would hunt again—always looking for that "prize kill"—the ferocious African cockroach stretching past the dreaded three inches in length! We drove away enjoying our victory.

Toward the end of February, Carol had to go home to Douala. I went with her because I needed to retrieve some helicopter parts still in airport customs in Douala. Steven and Colby stayed in Bamenda with a young missionary couple.

While I was in Douala, I received a phone call from Kaylene saying that Steve had telexed, giving me the OK to come and the date I should leave Cameroon. That made me happy, but I had misgivings about leaving the boys for so long. In the States, if anything were to go wrong, I could be called immediately, but that was not always possible in Africa. But I called the missionary couple watching the boys, and they agreed to keep them.

The next day was unbelievably stressful. I wanted to send Steve a mailgram to let him know I was coming, but the only girl at the post office who could send mailgrams was sick. I tried to reach him by telex through our Switzerland office, but that didn't work either. In the meantime I was running back and forth from the airport, dealing with uncooperative customs officials and trying to get the 101 signatures needed to retrieve a small box of helicopter parts.

In the afternoon I went to the ticket office of Ethiopian Airlines to purchase the ticket for Uganda. The girl at the desk said the young man who could help me would be back "in a moment," so I waited. When he finally arrived, he looked absolutely awful. He was shaking and sweating, and it was apparent he didn't belong at work. I told him what I wanted, and he asked me to come back later. At that moment, the assistant manager, dressed in street clothes and not his working uniform, came out of his office and asked what the problem was. The ticket agent told him and politely asked him if he could help. His brusque response startled both the ticket agent and me: "Hey, I'm not even supposed to be here!" Needless to say, I did not get my airline ticket that day.

It is amazing to watch the Lord work. What I was experiencing as total frustration was really an expression of His mercy. I did not know it at the time, but while I was trying unsuccessfully to get the ticket to Uganda Steve was in the process of final discussions with Ugandan officials concerning the role of our helicopter. Although every day the possibilities changed, during that day of extreme aggravation for me, Steve's plans were finalized. He was to leave Uganda, fly the helicopter to Kenya, and return to Cameroon. If I had gotten my ticket for Uganda that afternoon, a large sum of our money would have been lost in paperwork for months. Not only did God spare us from that further difficulty, I later realized that He was sparing us from being in Uganda during a time of tragedy when we both would have ached to have been back in Bamenda. But all that was in the future.

Late in the afternoon, by another telex, I learned that Steve was coming home in one week. I drove back to Bamenda to be with the boys, and they were very excited to hear that Daddy was coming home soon.

Four days later, on Sunday, March 1, I went back to Douala to pick up Steve and deliver some flyers for a large tent crusade the Full Gospel Mission was to be holding. I also had to clear yet another helicopter part through customs. Since it would be a quick trip with so much business involved, I decided to leave the boys with the missionary couple who had cared for them before. Steven and Colby were playing out front when I was ready to leave. I went over to say good-bye and suggested that we pray for Daddy to come home safely. Steven was more interested in what he was playing, but he said a prayer to make me happy. Colby shared a beautiful prayer and thanked Jesus for bringing his Daddy home. They promised to be good boys, and we kissed good-bye—and off I went to get my husband.

The next morning, I dropped off the flyers and headed over to the airport. To my surprise, my efforts at customs went incredibly well. I had that helicopter part in less than two hours. It had to be some sort of record. So I had nothing to do until Wednesday when Steve was due to arrive.

That evening, I stayed with Carol in her tiny one bedroom apartment in Douala. During the evening I began to feel sluggish, and my back started to bother me. While I was getting ready for bed, I noticed a rash developing on my legs and wondered what I had eaten to cause it. I mentioned the rash to Carol, who was a nurse, but she didn't know what it could have been since we had both eaten the same thing for dinner. Carol went to bed, and I went to sleep on the floor in a sleeping bag, without thinking any more about it. When I awoke the following morning, I discovered that the rash had spread over my entire body except for my face. However, since I was still able to function as usual, I ignored it and hoped it would soon go away. It didn't. By late afternoon, I was feverish and went back to the apartment. Not long after that I crawled into Carol's bed, and she took wonderful care of me that evening. I kept hoping I would be better in the morning because Steve was flying in then. I simply *had* to be better.

Unfortunately, by morning I had actually got worse. I was nauseated, my fever was up, and my rash was in full bloom. What a nice homecoming present I would be for Steve! I tried to comb my hair and kept telling myself that if I could just get out of bed, freshen up, and get some air I would be fine; but in fact, I was so sick I couldn't even muster the strength to go to the airport to meet him. A neighbor of mine from Bamenda, Pastor John Treherne, happened to be in Douala with his family, and he generously offered to get Steve.

When Steve walked in, the first thing he said as he gazed down at my pitiful performance of acting healthy was, "You look beautiful!" I didn't know whether to laugh or slug him.

He had brought me gifts from Uganda, and I gave him his welcome home present as well. It was a new wedding ring to replace the one he had accidentally thrown out of the jeep. I had bought the ring from a little street vendor, and it wasn't worth its weight in banana peels, but I wanted it to help start a romantic evening. Instead, we found that I had scarlet fever and that we had no place to spend the night, since Carol's place was so tiny. I really didn't care because I was so happy to have Steve home. Fortunately, we found a room at the Baptist Guest House and began to work on getting me well enough to make the five-hour jeep ride back to Bamenda. When Carol told us she was going to Bamenda the following day, we asked her to check on the kids while she was there and to let them know we were coming soon.

Thursday came, and I wasn't better, but worse—that beautiful rash all over my body had begun to itch. I couldn't believe one person could itch in so many places at one time. Steve went to the pharmacy, and they suggested some antihistamine pills and a tube of cream. He rubbed large amounts of the cream all over me and combined with the pills it was truly a healing balm. Thus donned from head to toe, I went with Steve to find a place to eat.

We ended up at a hotel restaurant near the guest house. We had a relaxing dinner as we caught up on all the news of each other's adventures. When the meal was over, Steve went over to talk to the waiter about something. At the same moment my itch started to attack again—viciously and unmercifully. I needed desperately to find a private place to *scratch!* There was no time to inform Steve of my plight, so I raced off and slipped out the nearest "sortie" (French for exit door). The sortie led to a dark stairwell, and with wild frenzy, I scratched and scratched while frantically trying to locate the cream hidden somewhere in the recesses of my purse. I was almost in tears by the time I found it. I struggled to get the cap off and furiously rubbed huge blobs of the stuff all over my body. I heard doors opening and shutting above my head, but at that point I didn't care if anyone found me acting like a "weird foreigner."

I don't know how long I spent in that dark stairwell, but when I came out, Steve was sitting in the front lounge area, and he didn't look very happy. The oddness of the situation made me laugh, but that seemed only to make him more upset because he had been very worried about me. I had literally disappeared and had not reappeared in a usual amount of time, and he hadn't known why. I must admit I was touched by his concern, but nothing could have stopped me from scratching that intolerable itch.

The next morning I felt much better, so we made plans to head back to Bamenda. As I was finishing up in the bathroom, the guest house manager came to tell us that we had a phone call. I couldn't imagine who it could be. A few minutes later Steve came into the room and told me to come to him.

"What?" I asked.

"Come and sit down on the bed. I have some bad news."

I felt confused and was caught off-guard by the way Steve was acting. But nothing could have prepared me for what he said next. As he held me in his arms, he said gently, "Colby drank some poison last night. He didn't survive."

14
New Creation

I cannot tell you what my first words were because I don't remember them. I do recall a brief moment of disbelief, but then I remembered Christina, and I knew death was real. I also knew that my husband was right there beside me, and it was he who had spoken the words. When the reality of those words began to sink in, all I could do was cry and wail and call out to God as Steve pulled me closer, holding me as tightly as he could.

"O God!" I cried. "Why two? Why do I have to give up two children?" I cried, and I cried, and I cried. The pain of sudden loss pierced my heart. Everything inside me called out to God for some kind of release.

I knew my cries could be heard throughout the guest house, and for that reason I was glad I was in Africa. Their custom upon hearing tragic news is to wail, moan, and cry out. I could not have grieved any other way. I believe with all my heart that the Africans can teach Americans much about mourning. Instead of saying, "OK, everything is under control here. I'm a missionary (or a pastor, or whatever)," why don't we admit the hurt and pain? When Job was stripped of everything he had, the pain was so great he cursed the day he was born and cried out to God. His questions were not ones doubting God's sovereignty. That was clear in his statement "The Lord gave and the Lord has taken away; may the name of the Lord be praised" (Job 1:21). His requests were for understanding and wisdom. He sought answers to explain the pain he had to bear.

It hurts to have someone you love ripped out of your life. That was my pain, my sorrow. Too many Christians believe that if they mourn outwardly, they are showing unbelief or weakness of character. Yet in my own experience, only through the release of those feelings of loss can God come in and begin healing the heart.

Dean was flying down in the helicopter to get us, so we got our things together, and the guest house driver took us to the airport to wait. The wait lasted forever. Steve was busy filing a flight plan and ordering fuel for the trip home, and I sat in the car with the driver, exhausted by the heat of the African sun and numb with pain. Steve came over to the car when he could, and we would hold each other, but I just kept thinking, *O God, why two? Why two? Is it something I've done?*

Dean arrived at noon. He and Steve talked for a few minutes, and then Dean came over to me. I started to cry immediately, and he held me and tried to share my grief.

The flight home was the most difficult we had ever made. For most of the trip we remained silent, and when someone did speak, the subject was insignificant and meaningless. We arrived in Bamenda at about 1:30 that afternoon and were greeted by many of the missionaries and the national community. The two people we wanted to see the most were the couple who had been taking care of the boys. Steve and I felt deeply for them, and our hearts ached to let them know we loved them. When I saw the young woman's face filled with tears, we grabbed each other and hugged and cried. Can you imagine how you would feel if a child you were taking care of died? Only God could fully comprehend that pain, but even in our limited, human way, Steve and I understood their suffering. We wanted to do all we could to help them know that we did not want our grief to be a hindrance to their healing.

We were led into Dean and Kaylene's living room, where decisions were made concerning Colby's burial. I depended so much on Steve for those decisions. I was still very sick, and I just wanted everyone else to do what they thought best. Things happen so differently in Africa, and within five minutes we had decided on services for that afternoon at 4:30. The community of believers got together and took care of all the details. Their doing so was a testimony to their loving character, and I was reminded of the New Testament church and how they cared for one another, meeting each other's needs.

A small group drove to the hospital to get Colby. Steve had not seen Colby for more than a month, and I wondered how he felt about having been away so long and having been excluded from Colby's last few weeks of life. I marveled at his tender and loving spirit as he and Pat Minerts, a missionary friend, prepared Colby for burial. Steve had brought back a new outfit from Kenya for Colby, and with much care he dressed Colby in it while Pat combed his hair and applied color to his cheeks.

In the meantime, people started to gather. A few minutes before the casket arrived, Steve came over to the couch and gently asked me if I wanted to see Colby before he was brought out for viewing. I was so weak physically that I didn't know if I could handle that emotionally, but I wanted to say good-bye to my little son and tell him I loved him. Steve took me into the bedroom. Colby was lying on a table by the closet. Those few precious moments holding his small hand were so special, and they were a necessary process for my heart. *My little Colby—good-bye. My little Colby—I love you. We love you.*

The Cameroonians practice open-casket services, which normally I wouldn't have minded, but in this instance I was afraid Colby's funeral would turn into a show to see the "white child." Kaylene was sensitive to my fears and kept ob-

131

servers from crowding in. The casket was placed on the hangar tarmac, with the helicopter just a few feet away. Moments later we all moved down the hillside of Helimission's compound to the grave site. The service itself was beautiful and comforting, but I couldn't help thinking back four years to the service for my daughter. I felt so strange—as though I were in a dream. Feelings of despair were crowding in, yet at the same time I sensed love from everyone around me. Feelings of helplessness overwhelmed me, yet I sensed a new beginning for Colby, and also for Steve, Steven, and me as a family. I remembered seeing the faces of some of our national neighbors peering through the fence and prayed that they would hear a message of hope amidst death. But at the same time I ached for Colby's death to be a lie.

On Friday, March 6, 1987, our little Colby was buried. Kaylene made a lovely flower arrangement from her garden, which she placed on the grave. She and Dean led Steve and me back to the house for a small reception, and an hour later we went home. The speed of it all overwhelmed me. So soon we were left alone with our grief.

The day after Colby's burial I started to get feverish, experienced chills, and became extremely weak. On Sunday our local congregation came over to the house to mourn and to show their respect. The women brought in some national food, and the men helped to set up chairs. While the women served the meal there were singing and words of comfort. Our national pastor, Pius, spoke movingly of the grief he felt in his heart for us. Many of the forty people present sat in silence. They stayed about two hours. Then they cleared the table, and each one came over to us, gave his or her final respects with a handshake or gentle nod of the head, and quietly left. It was a beautiful time of sharing with the national community in Bamenda and a beautiful expression of their love and compassion for us.

The next day I grew still worse. Steve took me to the hospital, where they ran a basic lab test. The results showed that, in addition to scarlet fever, I had malaria. The Cameroonian doctor gave me some oral medications, sent me home, and told me I would get better. My muscles ached so much from the malaria that as I lay in bed I was extremely restless, shifting constantly, fighting chills one moment and sweating profusely the next. It was so bad that Steve couldn't even sleep next to me but pulled up a small bed beside mine. Yet, as I lay there, praying earnestly for God to help—indeed, begging Him—a mosquito flew around my ear, taunting me with its buzzing.

That night after I had finally dozed off, I suddenly awoke with a sharp stinging pain under my collar bone. I slapped the area as hard as I could, but I had already been stung by a bee. That woke Steve, but when I told him what had happened, he didn't believe me. He assured me everything was OK and told me to go back to sleep. Within a few seconds his breathing was heavy and regular, and he slept soundly through the night while I lay awake, staring at the shadows on the wall and wondering what could possibly happen to me next. In the light of the morning hours I found that bee, dead on the sheets beside me, and proudly presented it to Steve—who then had to believe me.

As the day wore on my health showed little sign of improvement. *Where is the Lord?* I wondered. *Doesn't He hear my prayers? How much more can I take?* I was tired of being sick. The medicines should have been doing their job, freeing me to sort out my thoughts and feelings about Colby's death. I knew deep down that God was allowing the trials for a reason, yet at that point I felt so sick, so tired, and so discouraged I thought I would rather die and get it all over with.

Although malaria is a sure way to lose weight, the process is nauseating. By Thursday, I had become dehydrated and was still not responding to the medication, so I was hospitalized for an I V drip treatment. I lay in a hot, stuffy room on a bed of thin vinyl padding and was given a bottle of fresh water. By nightfall I could feel the healing effects of the Quinimax treatment flowing through my veins. Steve was absolutely wonderful as he cared for me there.

My illness was very difficult for the family, and Lil' Steven was a deep concern. Colby's death was so much for such a small heart to carry, yet God's grace and love were big enough to hold him. He was, in turn, a strong comfort to us with his childlike faith and gestures of love. He came to the hospital every day with his daddy to visit me, constantly chattering away. We knew that he missed his brother deeply—especially when he began to ask for a new sister.

After three days in the hospital, I was finally released. When I got home my friend Judy filled in the details surrounding Colby's death. She said that at about 5:00 in the evening on Thursday, March 5, Colby somehow found some dog shampoo our yard man, Thomas, had hidden under a fuel drum in the back of the garage just outside the front door of our home. That particular shampoo was very potent and was used in its diluted form to kill ticks on animals. As soon as he drank the shampoo, Colby ran into the house and began to throw up. Jonathan, the babysitter, quickly asked him what he had done. The answer wasn't really clear, so Jonathan hastily picked Colby up, took him outside, and in restrained urgency, asked Colby to *show* him what he had been doing. Colby, knowing he had done something wrong but not understanding the severity of it, showed him the bottle. When Jonathan saw what it was, he raced up the street to find a ride to the hospital, carrying Colby under his arm. They arrived at the emergency room within fifteen minutes from the time he had ingested the poison.

The medical staff began emergency procedures right away, but Colby never did anything with half a heart. He had probably drunk the poison because he was thirsty, and he certainly hadn't sipped it. Consequently, the liquid had penetrated deep into his lungs. In fact, the poison he drank was so potent that even if Colby had been in the United States, the doctors could not have done anything for him. The poison was strong enough to kill a dog in twenty-four hours if applied to the skin in full strength. Carol had rushed to the hospital as soon as she learned of Colby's situation. It was fitting that the

Lord sent Colby's "Aunty Miss Carol" to be with him during those last few hours. Throughout the evening she sang him songs and told him how much Jesus—and his Mommy and Daddy—loved him.

Pastor John Treherne, Judy's husband, came and spoke in his famous Donald Duck voice and asked Colby if he would like to see Amy (his five-year-old daughter). Colby nodded that he would, but it was the last thing he was able to acknowledge before slipping into a coma. He went very quietly, and by 2:30 A.M. he had become "a new creation" in the presence of Jesus, his Lord.

As I learned of that evening's events, I can only thank God He spared Steve and me the pain of being there. Yes, I would have loved to have been with Colby, but I think the Lord knew I couldn't have handled the guilt I would have felt if Colby had drunk the poison while I was at home—and then to have watched him die so quickly as I stood by, helpless to aid him and consumed with "if onlys."

Steve and I believed that we were greatly spared in another way. Everyone had begun trying to call us the moment they realized what Colby had done. Even the operators who knew of the situation tried through the night to reach us. One operator was so concerned she even called back to Bamenda to see if anyone had been able to reach us on another line. But it was only in those ten minutes before we were ready to leave the guest house Friday morning that our friends were able to get a line straight through from Bamenda to Douala. We believed that God's timing in that circumstance was unmistakable. We would have felt nothing but devastation had we known Thursday night what was happening in Bamenda, for we could not have helped in any way or have reached Bamenda before Colby died. All we could have done was wait in utter helplessness. It would have been too much for our hearts to bear.

The actual fact of what Colby had done did not surprise us at all. Colby was one of those little boys who was into everything. Once during a six-week period he pulled a cast iron fence out of a cement porch, pulled the rubber bumper off our jeep, stuck firewood down the water reserve tank that brought water into the house by a pump, colored an entire wall, pulled more than a hundred carrots out of our garden and then tried to hide them by stuffing them through the chain link fench to the other side, brushed a paint roller, wet with leftover blue paint, over my freshly painted yellow kitchen walls so that he could "be like Mommy." We spanked him, we put him in the corner, we lectured him, we gave him more attention, we prayed over him. But nothing seemed to help.

After praying over him one night, Steve came up with the idea of using food to reward and punish Colby. More than anything else in the world that boy loved to eat, so we decided to try it, but only when Colby had destroyed something or had done something that could have hurt himself or someone else. By the time Steve left for Uganda, Colby was doing beautifully. The entire month before his death, he had begun to understand what behaviors we were trying to change, and we did not have to discipline him nearly so much as before. We knew that Colby had not been acting maliciously or out of rebelliousness; rather, his behavior seemed to be the natural result of his curiousity.

Over the next few days Steve and I tried to write a newsletter to let our friends and supporters know about Colby. I began the letter by explaining the events as they took place, starting with my trip to Douala to pick up Steve. As I told what happened and put our feelings on paper, I felt the love of God surrounding me, and I knew I was being held in His grace as I wrote.

> God is Sovereign, and I cannot even begin to share the love I feel for Him in my heart at this moment. I praise Him for His wisdom, His grace, and His faithfulness. Do you see what this world offers? Death, sickness, and heartache; and all because of the curse of sin. . . . Where is our hope unless it is in Christ Jesus our Lord? Where else in this world are we offered new life? For Jesus said, "I am the

resurrection and the life. He who believes in me will live, even though he dies" (John 11:25). Is there any other God that offers such love? "For God so loved the world (you), that he gave his one and only Son"—He died to lift the curse of sin from man—"that whosoever believes in Him shall not perish but have eternal life" (John 3:16). The gospel of Christ is good news!

Oh, how we love and miss our Colby, but we do have this hope: "We . . . would prefer to be away from the body and at home with the Lord" (2 Corinthians 5:8). These are not just words on paper. We *shall* see our Colby again, and cry no more.

Steve's note began with the bewilderment we both had felt:

Initially, I was very bitter and angry with God. We had obeyed the commission of Jesus to follow Him, we had relied on His promises: "No one who has left home . . . for the sake of the kingdom of God will fail to receive many times as much in this age" (Luke 18:29-30). We had put our trust in Him: "I will say of the Lord, 'He is my refuge and my fortress, my God, in whom I trust.' . . . He will command his angels concerning you to guard you in all your ways; they will lift you up in their hands, so that you will not strike your foot against a stone. You will tread upon the lion and the cobra" (Psalm 91:2, 11-13). Yet again, "And these signs will accompany those who believe . . . when they drink deadly poison, it will not hurt them at all" (Mark 16:17-18).

Then Steve applied his own personal reading of a passage in Matthew to the situation with Colby. In the Scripture passage the disciples rebuked those who brought the little children to Jesus to be blessed, but the Lord chastised the disciples for doing so, saying, "Let the little children come to me, and do not hinder them, for the kingdom of heaven belongs to such as these" (Matthew 19:13-14). In Steve's para-

137

phrase the wording was changed considerably, though the message that the kingdom belonged to such as Colby remained the same:

> The Lord gently chastised me as He did with the disciples, "Then the angels brought little Colby unto Jesus for him to place his hands on him and pray for him. But I (Steve) rebuked the angels for failing to protect Colby. Jesus said, 'Let Colby come to me, and do not hinder him, for the kingdom of heaven belongs to such as him'" (Matthew 19:13-14, freely paraphrased).
>
> It is hard to accept the word of God sometimes because we don't understand. It hurts so much to be without one whom we have loved so much.
>
> Colby's favorite song was "He's Still Working on Me," and he would sing it with great enthusiasm and encouragement. Now, I must accept that although "He's still working on me," He has completed His work in Colby, and has called him to a grander task within His almighty kingdom.
>
> I must thank the Lord for allowing us to be a part of Colby's life, and to share in his happiness as well as his sorrows. "Though the fig tree does not bud and there are no grapes on the vines, though the olive crop fails and the fields produce no food, though there are no sheep in the pen and no cattle in the stalls, [though my son and my daughter die] . . . yet I will rejoice in the Lord, I will be joyful in God my Savior. The Sovereign Lord is my strength; he makes my feet like the feet of a deer, he enables me to go on the heights" (Habakkuk 3:17-19).

God began to heal Steve and me. We started to understand that as we simply trusted Him, no matter what the circumstance, He would build our faith and enable us to offer hope to the world around us. Our task was to hold onto the Word we had been taught and to believe that the death of our little Colby was a part of the plan God had from eternity to bring mankind unto himself through Jesus Christ.

We were believing God for the strength we needed to move forward, but our outward circumstances were not encouraging, for less than a week after I got out of the hospital Steve, too, developed malaria. The doctor decided to put him in the hospital right away rather than risk his not responding to treatment. For the next two days, Steve lay in the same hospital bed I had, looking about as pitiful as I had remembered feeling, and my heart went out to him.

African hospitals do not have paid dieticians in cute uniforms coming around to ask you which entrée you prefer. Instead, the only food you get is the food your relatives or friends bring you. I still didn't feel like cooking, and Steve certainly didn't feel like eating, but I attempted to make his entrées as palatable as possible. Despite his lack of appetite, Steve was out of the hospital in two days and appeared to regain his strength within twenty-four hours. In fact, he regained his health so quickly that if I had asked him to run laps around the compound, he probably would have done so—if only to prove he could. I was envious of his quick recovery!

The three daily trips to the hospital to care for Steve totally drained me. Soon I was back in bed, struggling to get better with the aid of pills and a putrid vitamin drink the doctor had prescribed, and Steve was back to waiting on me. What were we in for next?

15
Release

Each day the following week I could feel strength draining from me like a slow leak in a life-raft. But I was determined to ignore the deterioration because we had received a call from my parents telling us they were coming to Africa. I was thrilled. This was a time when I just "wanted my mommy."

My parents' trip had come about in an unusual way. One night shortly after Colby's death, my mother was pacing through her trailer—confused, angry, and aching to be with us. In her anguish she cried out, "Lord, I want to be with my daughter!" almost demanding that God answer her. Still, she saw no chance of overcoming the obstacles of thousands of miles and thousands of dollars. Twenty minutes later she received a phone call from my sister-in-law, who told her what she would need to do if she ever had to get passports and visas in a hurry. My mother wrote down the information but thought it would never be needed. My father called a few minutes later from work and confirmed her feelings when he expressed wariness about going overseas.

Over the next several days, the people living in their retirement community, The Windward Isles, in Sarasota, Florida, got together and collected more than $5,000 for my parents so they could make the trip. My parents were stunned. The doors were flying open. But my father still had serious misgivings about going, for he was concerned about the dangers Americans were facing when they traveled overseas. His concerns were real. Terrorists were bombing airports, holding American hostages, and even killing some. My mother tried to resign herself to his decision, but she prayed that the Lord would change my father's mind.

My parents called us the day after the money was raised, while I was sick with malaria. Steve talked to them at length, and his pain over Colby's death was obvious as he struggled with the promises of God that didn't seem to be holding true for us now. My parents, believing that we could use the money raised for them, asked him if we could possibly come back to the States for a while. Steve thought I might be able to go after I was well and that I could bring Steven, but he knew that he himself wouldn't be able to get away so easily. At that point in the conversation Steve tried to bring me to the phone, but my illness overcame me and he had to put me back to bed. When the conversation ended no decisions had been made.

After the call my father sat thinking quietly. He was deeply moved by our commitment to stay and serve the Lord through our tragedy and pain. Finally, he said two words: "Let's go." From then on God worked miraculously to bring all the details together. Steve and I prepared with great anticipation, but waiting for news of their final arrival date was frustrating. There were many "little" hassles to overcome before they could leave for Cameroon. The visa office in Washington for Cameroon required much detailed paperwork and many rubber-stamped signatures from every possible official. The waiting was made more difficult because I continued to deteriorate physically. I began to get low-grade fevers during the evening, but I would take aspirin and they would go away. I worried that I might not be able to make the trip to Douala to pick up my parents, but when the day finally came I pushed aside the fact that I was actually very sick.

Steve, Steven, and I drove down to Douala early on the day of their arrival, and we checked in for the evening at "The Seaman's Mission," a place for sailors to get a bed on land and a clean shower. We enjoyed the mission because it provided a pool as well as the most tender meat brochettes in Cameroon.

My parents' flight was late in arriving that evening, and while we waited in the airport restaurant, my fever went up again. When we saw their plane land at the end of the long terminal we went over to a railing that let us see down into the customs and baggage area, hoping to get a glimpse of them. I became extremely dizzy while standing there and finally had to sit on the floor to keep from fainting. Eventually Steve caught sight of my parents and helped me downstairs so that we could greet them. After a long battle through customs they pushed their way through the crowd. My mother hugged me hard, looked me over, and said, "Boy, am I glad to see you! You look like death warmed over!"

"Thanks, Mom. I love you too." But she was right. As much as I had tried to hide my pale face behind makeup, there are some things you just can't hide from your mother. Next was my dignified father. His embrace was strong and filled with compassion. I had never thought I would be hugging him in the hot, tropical city of Douala, Cameroon, West Africa. After warm hugs for Steve and Lil' Steven, we drove through town while they told us about the events of their trip. Lil' Steven could hardly keep still as he waited eagerly to see what Grandma and Grandpa had brought him.

We spent the night at the mission and then crammed into our little Russian jeep the following morning. We worked our way out of the city through busy streets and onto the long, winding road that led home. My parents were impressed by the size of the potholes we had and couldn't believe how many were so big we actually had to leave the road to avoid them. The trip was quite an adventure for them.

About halfway to Bamenda we stopped in a little village called Kekem. Almost all of the bush taxis traveling to and from Douala stopped there so that the passengers could eat and stretch their legs. The bush taxis were crammed full of people, animals, and countless bundles of "stuff," filling every nook and cranny and even piled high on top of the taxis. Sometimes, it looked as if the "stuff" would cause the tires to burst. The people traveling in the taxis needed more than just a stretch—they needed to be peeled apart, shaken out, and hung to dry.

In Kekem we visited the Cameroonian version of a fast food restaurant where hot pepe meat sticks were sold hot off the grill. We ordered the meat sticks without the hot pepe sauce. While they were cooking, my father asked the "chef" if he could take a picture of him preparing our food over the makeshift grills. The Africans are very industrious people, always looking for a way to make a franc. The chef agreed on the condition that my dad pay him for the privilege of placing his "skill" on film; however, once we actually tasted the meat sticks, we found the meat remarkably tough and very stringy. We were somewhat discouraged by that, but we settled for some baked bread and warm cokes instead. So far, my parents had not been overawed by our life-style. My father's opinion only grew worse when he saw that the outdoor potty was at the side of the very busy, very congested marketplace.

We left Kekem and headed into the higher hills of the northwest province, where my parents were notably relieved by the cooler weather. They were surprised when we reached our compound to find that we didn't live in a mud hut or bathe in the river. We had electricity (sometimes) and running water (sometimes) and flush toilets (most of the time) and a cook (almost all of the time). My mother especially liked John and couldn't believe that we only paid him $100 a month to work six days a week. He not only cooked, he did the laundry by hand in the tub, cleaned the house, washed the floors with a tick solution, did much of my open marketing, and even babysat the kids when Steve and I flew into the bush areas together.

Two days later, I went back to the hospital to try to find out what was wrong with me. The fevers had been coming earlier in the day and were reaching a higher degree each time. And they were making me very tired. I did not want to be sick the entire time my parents were there. They had come halfway around the world to be with us, and it didn't take long to discover that my father wanted to convince us to come back home to the States—and he intended to succeed. "Haven't you had enough?" he asked.

I could understand how he felt. When news of the disaster of Lake Nyos hit their local newspaper in Florida, the headline simply read, "2,000 Dead in Bamenda." That frightened my mother terribly because when she thought of an African village she certainly didn't think of one so large that two thousand people lived in it. She relaxed only when she was able to reach us by phone the following afternoon. Then they had received the news of Steve's arrest in Uganda while the boys and I were alone in Cameroon. Colby's death only increased their conviction that we shouldn't be in Africa. They wanted their only daughter and her family back in the United States where they thought we belonged.

All of that was running through my mind when the doctor called me into his office, sat me down in front of his desk, and said, "I can't find anything wrong with you. The malaria test came up negative. I think it's stress." He gave me four more prescriptions for the putrid vitamin drink I so disliked and told me to "go home, go to bed, and get better." I left his office confused and depressed.

On the drive home, I fought back tears. *OK, Lord*, I grumbled. *I admit that I have been under an unusual amount of strain lately. But if I have to "go home, go to bed, and get better" all on my own, it's going to take forever considering the way I feel!* A friend of mine had mailed me a book shortly before about a woman in Christian ministry who collapsed from too much pressure. The lady in the book had to stay in bed for six weeks before she regained her strength. The thought that I might have to do the same sickened me—and then to have to tell my parents that my fatigue and fevers were due to *stress*. They had flown halfway around the world to convince us to come home because of our life-style. The doctor's diagnosis would only confirm their thinking.

When we arrived home, Steve put a foam mattress on the living room floor so that I could be part of what was going on. We told my parents what the doctor had said, and they did their best to comfort me in every way. Yet each day the fever went higher. Still, in spite of the illness, Steve and I strongly felt the call of God to stay where we were, and as we watched, a beautiful thing happened. After only a few days, my parents recognized God's call as well. They experienced with us daily our commitment to share Christ's love through the helicopter, they experienced the simple joys of family life in the bush, and they met several of our missionary friends—normal people wanting to serve Jesus where they could bring Him the most glory. My parents quickly appreciated that we were completely satisfied with the knowledge that God had placed us there and that we were doing exactly what He wanted us to do. As Christians, my parents were sensitive to see God's hand in our lives. I do not think many parents could have accepted God's will for their children so easily, especially when it was evident that their children were suffering as a result of their obedience.

One Wednesday afternoon, just after the noon meal when everyone was taking a nap, my fever peaked. A fever of that nature makes a person delirious, and I felt myself sinking into self-pity. I started to lose control of my thoughts, and nausea overwhelmed me. All my joints ached, and my muscles tightened. In desperation I called for John to wake my mother. She came out of the bedroom, and I tried to explain to her what was happening. I didn't know what else to do but beg her to read me some Scripture. She took the Bible from the coffee table, sat down next to me on the floor, and for more than an hour read psalm after psalm after psalm to me. With closed eyes I listened to the truth and beauty of the words, and soon I could feel warm tears running down my cheeks, each psalm reminding me that there were still many areas of my life I had not given to Jesus. The words cut deep into my spirit.

O Lord, do not rebuke me in your anger
    or discipline me in your wrath.
For your arrows have pierced me,
    and your hand has come down upon me.
Because of your wrath there is no health in my body;
    my bones have no soundness because of my sin.
My guilt has overwhelmed me
    like a burden too heavy to bear.

My wounds fester and are loathsome
    because of my sinful folly.
I am bowed down and brought very low;
    all day long I go about mourning.
My back is filled with searing pain;
    there is no health in my body.
I am feeble and utterly crushed;
    I groan in anguish of heart.

All my longings lie open before you, O Lord;
    my sighing is not hidden from you.
My heart pounds, my strength fails me;
    even the light has gone from my eyes.
                   (Psalm 38:1-11)

Yet, in God's tender mercy, so much of what she read was a healing balm to my soul. God's Word allowed me to put my focus back on Jesus and to forget about myself and my circumstances. Peace flowed through my entire body, my mind cleared, and I released my heart to the Lord.

Cleanse me with hyssop, and I will be clean;
    wash me, and I will be whiter than snow.
Let me hear joy and gladness;
    let the bones you have crushed rejoice.
Hide your face from my sins
    and blot out all my iniquity.

147

Create in me a pure heart, O God,
and renew a steadfast spirit within me.
Do not cast me from your presence
or take your Holy Spirit from me.
Restore to me the joy of your salvation
and grant me a willing spirit, to sustain me.
(Psalms 51:7-12)

16
The Choice

We decided that whatever I had could not have been simply stress. Because I was too embarrassed to go back to the national doctor, I elected to go to the Baptist Mission Hospital in Banso, about two hours' drive away. As we were leaving, Dean called and asked if Steve could come down to the hangar for a few minutes. The interruption brought up in me a spurt of anger. Why did he have to bring up some last minute detail?

But then Steve returned. A telex had arrived from Switzerland: we were to move to Ethiopia. Dean had given Steve the news in the hanger rather than at our home because he knew how sick I was. He didn't want to weaken my physical condition even further by making a sudden announcement of the new posting. When I heard that, I prayed that God would forgive me for my quick judgments and bless Dean and Kaylene for their loving Christian friendship throughout our trials.

Actually, the thought of moving didn't bother me. Steve and I had got used to being moved around during our days in the military, though I couldn't see how we could move in the immediate future since my plans were only to get to the hospital and get well.

We climbed into the combi-van and headed for Banso. My parents were not impressed by the dirt road on which we had to travel, but the beauty of the countryside made up for much of their discomfort. Dry season was upon us, so by the time we reached Banso Baptist Hospital, we were covered from head to toe with orange dust and dirt. My mother looked like the redhead she had always dreamed of being. It took two very vigorous scrubbings to get the dirt out of our hair and scalps. My father kept asking me, "This is wonderful, right? That's what you kept writing to me—that Africa was wonderful? This is it, isn't it? Wonderful?"

My appointment was for the following morning with Dr. Money. He did a very detailed examination, although I suspected he already knew what he was dealing with. He looked at the blood work himself and, indeed, found that I had malaria again, a strain resistant to the medications I had been taking. He also discovered that I had become anemic, so he put me on an aggressive treatment to try to wash the disease completely out of my system.

Dr. Money wanted me to stay in the guest house next to the hospital for at least three days. Everyone was less than thrilled to hear that, for all we had brought with us was one change of clothes apiece and a small amount of food, but we dutifully checked in.

During the three days we stayed at the guest house my parents explored Banso thoroughly and experienced more of life in the bush. My father later told me of their visit to the open market, where everything from pots and pans to shoes and cows' livers were sold, and of their experience with fufu and jamajama, two national foods.

Fufu is made out of ground cornmeal cooked over a fire in a large pot placed on three rocks. After the cornmeal is cooked and while it is still very hot, it is formed into shapes resembling potato cakes. One eats fufu by scooping a small portion at a time with two fingers and then dipping it into a meat soup. The consistency of fufu is like stiff mashed potatoes that have cooled. If it were thrown against the wall it would probably stick. It doesn't taste bad if it is hot and properly prepared so it isn't gritty, and I think my mother enjoyed it, but I know that once fufu has cooled, it has the consistency of paste. Jamajama is a green leafy vegetable that reminded me of wimpy, soggy collard greens.

One of my mother's biggest shocks came one evening when we were invited by a mission doctor for dinner. The cook had not allowed enough time to prepare the pork, and the doctor asked if we would mind if we had something else. My mother jokingly said, "Oh, just put it in the microwave." With a puzzled look on her face, the doctor said, "Can you do that? I've never been taught how to cook meat in a microwave. Come and show me!" Needless to say, my mother couldn't believe the doctor had a microwave in her African bush home. She showed the doctor how to cook the meat, and twenty minutes later we sat down to nice pork dinner.

My dad found great joy in being able to watch his favorite football game on video cassette. The best part was that he already knew the outcome. Now I hate football (and baseball, and basketball, etc.), and one of the reasons I was glad to be in Africa was that there was no Monday Night Football (or football any other night), yet I was happy to see my parents getting such a kick out of modern gadgets in the bush of northern Cameroon.

My mother also toured the hospital. She had been an emergency room supervisor for many years in a large city hospital, but nothing she experienced there prepared her for what she saw in the bush of Cameroon. The beds were full and crowded into large rooms. Many of the patients had brought their own mats so that they could sleep on the floor, and they were accompanied by family members who stayed with them and prepared their meals, doubling or tripling the number of people in the hospital. Mother found whole families with some patients. They had brought everything they owned with them and slept outside on the hospital grounds.

The medical doctors had extra obstacles blocking their attempts to treat the bush people because of the people's beliefs in the ju-ju, or witch doctor. The ju-ju used plants, natural roots, leaves, and seeds to help heal some of the villagers' problems. Many of the patients put their trust in the village ju-ju until they had almost reached the point of death. Then in desperation they sought the help of "the white man's medicine," but often—even if they were diagnosed quickly and without difficulty—it was too late. If the patient died, the people said it was because the white man's medicine did not work. The ju-ju would boast that the white man's medicine was evil. It was hard to show the villagers that the power of the plants, roots, and leaves lay not in the ju-ju or in his magic, but in the God who created those medicines for man's benefit and use. When they were used properly, their healing powers could be exercised by any man.

My mother did not see walls painted in soft colors with beautifully framed pictures by famous artists as she made her rounds, but she did see a dedicated medical team who cared deeply for the people. Many of them were nationals who had been given the privilege of going to school and obtaining nursing degrees. And she saw that even under the most primitive conditions, the patients were treated, healed, and sent home.

But that afternoon when Steve put me to bed and made me a sandwich, I was not thinking about life in Africa and all that was new and distinct about it. I felt sorry for myself. I did not want to go through another five days of fighting to get better, of swallowing eight or nine pills at a time, or of suffering the inevitable effects of the anti-malaria medicine—a loud ringing in the ears.

Soon my fever peaked again. The chills and the sweats plagued me, making one more brutal attack before the medicines could begin to fight the war inside my body. Steve and my parents had gone out for a breath of fresh air, and when Steve came back into the room he found me almost delirious. In desperation I asked him to read some Scriptures, remembering how that had helped me before. As he read, one of the passages reminded me of the verse in Philippians I had longed to know personally, the verse the Lord had given me when I questioned Him about coming to the mission field: "I want to know Christ and the power of His resurrection and the fellow-ship of sharing in his sufferings, becoming like him in his death, and so, somehow, to attain to the resurrection from the dead" (Philippians 3:10).

Now, as I lay there on the bed looking at my husband as he read, I thought about that verse. How could the death of our two children, my extreme illness, the daily hardships we endured while serving the Lord, and even that bee sting reveal to me what the verse was saying? How could the verse relate to me? How could our experiences compare in any way with what Jesus Christ suffered for me on the cross? "Lord, please, show me," I prayed.

At that moment, I felt God speak clearly and gently, but firmly, to my heart: "Kathy, it is not *what* you are suffering that makes any difference but *how* you are able to go through your suffering, as difficult as it may be, as Christ endured His."

Immediately, as I received those words, a picture of Jesus came to mind, and I could see the difference only too clearly. The Scriptures say that Jesus went as quietly as a lamb, without complaint, accepting what the Father willed as perfect. My own sufferings will never compare with what Christ did for me, but Jesus trusted the Father with His very life to show me how deeply He loved me. When I realized that, there was nothing left to question concerning His love. I knew that I had not submitted completely to my suffering as God's perfect will for my life.

As with Christina's and Colby's death, my malaria was part of God's eternal plan for my life. The issue was simply, was I going to trust Christ, or wasn't I? Were the truths and stories I'd been taught about Him all my life simply words on paper, or were they truly words of life and hope that applied to me?

> Count it pure joy, my brothers, whenever you face trials of many kinds. (James 1:2)

153

I consider that our present sufferings are not worth comparing with the glory that will be revealed in us. (Romans 8:18)

And the God of all grace, who called you to his eternal glory in Christ, after you have suffered a little while, will himself restore you and make you strong, firm and steadfast. (1 Peter 5:10)

Put another way, was I going to take my eyes off my circumstances and look to Jesus? I knew that if I didn't do so my sufferings and circumstances would overwhelm me. Without that trust in Jesus I would have no hope, and there would be no difference between me and an unbeliever.

It was my choice to make, for the Lord had directed me with His Word. As I meditated on the Scriptures and as Steve and I talked about how Christ works in our lives, the Lord gently allowed me to release my suffering to Him, and within twenty minutes I began to feel better and more optimistic than I had in days. I took my temperature, but my fever had not changed at all. In fact, nothing about my physical condition had changed. I still had the chills. I still had the sweats. The difference was in my attitude and in my ability to give my circumstances completely over to the Lord without complaint, accepting what the Father willed as perfect. When I did that, I could endure my suffering with all joy. "My comfort in my suffering is this: Your promise preserves my life" (Psalm 119:50).

Having been a Christian for years, I should have known that already. Actually, the Lord had been teaching me and teaching me well, and I know He had enabled me to trust Him through much testing and trial even up to that time. Yet in Colossians 2:2 Paul prays that "they may have the *full* riches of *complete* understanding, in order that they may *know* the mystery of God, namely, Christ, in whom are hidden all treasures of wisdom and knowledge" (emphasis added). God, in His unsearchable wisdom, desires that I know Him intimately. His love for me is so strong and His desire for my perfection so great that, as it says in Hebrews 4:12, He causes His Word to divide soul and spirit. What I had once understood only with my mind the Lord wanted me to make the lifeblood of my heart. God did not want me to live with just cold head knowledge but rather desired that more and more the character and mind of Jesus would become a natural part of who I was. The verse in Hebrews goes on to say that the Word judges the thoughts and attitudes of the heart, and I knew that was taking place in my heart on that day, in that African hospital bed.

Once I was willing to accept God's plan and completeness in my life, I was free to allow Him to heal the pain in my heart, but that caused His Word to divide even more sharply as suddenly I faced head-on the guilt I felt over Christina's and Colby's deaths. Although I thought I had come to an understanding concerning God's perfect plan and although I wanted to trust Him, my old nature wanted the guilt to cling to me like wet ashes on doused firewood. Whether it is intentional or not, our natural instinct is to blame someone for death. Oftentimes, we choose to blame ourselves. During the next few weeks, the Lord would be faithful to show me His Word, giving me a more complete understanding of the struggle with guilt.

After three days of treatment I began to regain health and strength, so we headed back to Bamenda. Two short days later we took my parents back to Douala and said our goodbyes. Lil' Steven was very sorry to see them go. Grandpa had brought a bat and ball for him and had taught him how to play, and Grandma had spoiled him at every opportunity. But now we had to begin preparations for our move to Ethiopia.

Before we left Cameroon, we had a grave marker made for Colby. We hired a young man to make a cement block, and while it was still wet, I carved the inscription into it with a big, black nail. It looked a little crude, but it fit quite naturally into the simplicity of the culture and the coarse terrain. The marker would be a constant reminder to others that there is a precious cost of furthering our Lord's gospel. I went away that afternoon sensing that we had a new beginning before us and wrote in my prayer journal:

April 29, 1987

My God . . . how you fill my heart with joy and peace. The house without Colby is extremely quiet and still. I miss him so much, Lord. It's not that I don't trust your decision, I just plain miss him and my heart overwhelms me when I think of how he died, how fast it was, that I wasn't there and that I couldn't tell him I loved him just one more time. Lord, please see my tears and love for Colby, and share my heart with him as you see him each day. I know that he understands now that we were not perfect parents, but we did so love him. I can't explain or express the pain I have in missing him, yet you know, Lord, I do not want to be selfish. I need to release him completely, my memories, my pain, and my total heart into your keeping.

The night is the worst time. As I lie on my bed, my mind races through so many thoughts and feelings. I struggle to seek your peace so that a spirit of fear does not enter. That even with Steve and Steven, I must release them to you and trust you with my heart if you should so decide to take them too. Do not let fear enter my heart, O Lord, for perfect love casts out fear. Pour your perfect love into me in such a way that I can understand it and put it to use.

It is not so much his physical death that bothers me, but the loneliness I feel in missing him. Colby is not here. I miss him. I miss his hugs, his kisses, his sweet innocent prayers, his "He's still working on me," his "realiest" and "I'm the faaastest!" his beautiful blue eyes, blond hair, charm, and adorable face. Does he still love to eat? Thank you, Lord, for teaching me love through Colby.

Father, cover my family in your love. Your wisdom will guide our lives through suffering or joy. We must always trust you in that. I fear you because you are powerful and holy, and I long to please you, yet my weakness and aptitude for failure seem always before me. Father, please . . . Lord, please . . . forgive me. Help me to become as angry about sin as you are. It cost you the life of your Son. It must now cost me my will.

Revive my soul, Lord. You alone are the Holy One, the Healer of my heart.

The physical healing of the Lord continued so speedily that within a month of the time I was released from the hospital, we had packed our entire house, sold what we could, got our exit visas, completed our many customs checks, said our farewells, and traveled to Addis Ababa, Ethiopia, to meet our director, Ernie Tanner, and Larry, the new copilot and mechanic for our helicopter.

Steve and I believed the move would be good for us. I remembered that we had moved only one week after Christina had died, and I thought of how the Lord calls us to "press on toward the goal to win the prize for which God has called [us] heavenward in Christ Jesus" (Philippians 3:14). We could not dwell in the past but continually had to learn from it. Steve and I were looking toward the future with great anticipation and a renewed vision as we entered a famine-stricken country to help in whatever way we could.

17
Ethiopia

Since Steve and I were on the field full-time, we rarely saw other members of our mission. So we were delighted to see our director as we came out of the airport terminal. Ernie came to help us become acquainted with our new environment and to set us up in an apartment in Addis Ababa, which was to be our home for the next several months.

As we started the customs process, Ernie stopped us from writing down our occupation as "missionaries" on our entry cards. Unaccustomed to communist controls we hadn't realized that the designation *missionary* might pose a threat to them and keep us from entering the country. We quickly tore up our first entry cards and filled out two more, which stated that we would be working for the Relief and Rehabilitation Commission, a government office overseeing restoration to the famine-stricken areas.

As we drove away from the airport and into the city of Addis Ababa (known simply as Addis by its inhabitants), we saw a mixture of the old and new world. Big modern buildings erected before the revolution rose high into the air, while nestled among them were innumerable, shabby lean-tos with women working diligently outside washing laundry in rusty fuel barrels. The communist government proclaimed itself with colorful street banners, flags, monuments, and lights. On the main road we passed under large arches on which appeared the proclamations "Long Live Proletarianism" and "Workers of the World Unite." There were large billboards picturing the fathers of Communism: Marx, Engels, and Stalin. We soon came to a great "Fathers of Communism" intersection, and Ernie explained that it was Revolution Square, the site of a massive uprising eleven years earlier when Communists fought to tighten their grip. On one side of the square was a large stadium where all public functions were held. Ernie told us we would be living about two blocks from the square, so I began to look at the buildings more closely as we drove through the busy streets.

It did not take long for me to realize that Ernie was driving past all the beautiful buildings. Then I saw it. I knew he was going to take me to *that* building. I knew it. It reminded me of the overcrowded apartment buildings we had seen lining the streets of Manila in the Philippines. I thought, *No, Lord, not that one*. But I knew in my heart that that was it. My mind wandered back to the beauty and splendor of the tropical Cameroonian countryside. I needed to make an immediate adjustment.

We arrived hungry and tired from the all-night flight to an apartment building decorated with laundry hanging from every balcony and a "Tele Bar" on the ground floor. Our parking area was a dirt lot lined with lean-tos and filled with small children playing.

Inside we found a badly clogged sink, a cracked toilet seat, broken light bulbs, a stove in need of repair, and walls painted in an assortment of colors that lured me into the main living area for further investigation. The room was oddly shaped and painted most imaginatively. One wall was pale pink, one sea green, one brick gold, and one dirty white. The material used to cover the two chairs and the couch confused the eye still more: the pattern of the material used to upholster them was the same but the colors were different: one chair was earth brown and one was olive green, and the couch was a dirty ivory. It was going to take a lot of work and even more imagination to make the apartment feel like a home.

We were to stay at a guest house for a few days until the apartment was ready for us. I kept saying to Steve, in an attempt to convince myself, "I just need some sleep, and it won't be so bad. Everything always seems magnified when you're tired. Besides, housing is very difficult to get in Ethiopia. The government has strict control over it. Some people have looked for months—but maybe they just have an aversion to living in a kaleidoscope."

Five days later we moved in, having unclogged the sink, replaced the light bulbs, painted the kitchen, fixed the stove, and hung countless things on the living room walls to divert the eye. We never did get around to fixing that broken toilet seat. Priorities, I guess.

We did not have water every day because it had to be rationed to different sections of the city. The days we had water, I washed the laundry in the tub early in the morning. Sometimes I heard the water come on in the middle of the night, so I'd run in and fill the tub to make sure we had a full supply of water the next day. Eventually we made the apartment our haven of rest. We found a girl to help me with the chores so that I could teach Steven his lessons in the mornings. Things really weren't so bad. Once the apartment became our "home," we began to see all the good qualities it had to offer us. God was always faithful to supply our needs.

Steve was busy flying immediately. The demand for the helicopter in Ethiopia was much greater than in Cameroon because of the serious needs of the Ethiopian people. I wasn't able to fly with Steve as often as before because the helicopter was smaller than the one we had had in Cameroon and because the copilot, Larry, had to be on every flight to build up his flight experience. As a result, Steven and I were left at home a good deal, usually without transportation. We began to explore our surroundings on foot, finding the closest markets and fruit stands.

161

No sooner had we got settled in the apartment than Steve came home with a letter telling us we were being evicted. The government wanted the apartment. We had six weeks to leave. The Lord had been teaching me a greal deal over the past several months, so I was determined to see the eviction as a blessing in disguise. Maybe we could move to the outskirts of town onto a missionary compound and establish some friendships. Maybe we could find a home where all the walls were one color. Maybe we could move into a place with a flush toilet that worked more than three days a week. Now that would be a blessing!

We sent out the word that we were in need of housing, and everyone offered to help us find something. One couple said that if we really got stuck we could have a one-bedroom apartment their mission used. At least it was something, and we felt better about that.

After a couple of days of searching, we heard of a house at the Baptist compound outside of town. Our friends Wally and Tannie Eshenaur suggested that we put in a letter of request for the house. It seemed perfect for our needs: three bedrooms, a yard for Steven, friends his age next door, and a place for the Doberman pinscher puppy Steve had brought home to raise as our guard dog. We quickly submitted a letter. Still, the chance of our getting the home seemed impossible, especially since we were ninth on the list of applicants. In a communist country that might as well have been ninety-ninth. Yet if God intended for us to have the house, we knew it was possible. So we waited.

In the meantime, we were enjoying the Ethiopian people and culture. The people were incredibly friendly and hospitable. They were quick to smile, and it was a joy to talk with them. At the same time it was sad to see the streets lined with so many lame, blind, diseased, poor, and malnourished people—all begging for money. Steven and I had to walk up to the mission guest house for lunch every day, and we always took a pocketful of change with us, since a small amount of change meant a plate of food for the people lining the road. It never seemed to be quite enough, but they came to expect us and always gave us a respectful greeting and thank you. At first we gave toys to the children, but when we learned their parents had to sell the toys to buy food, we stopped offering toys and continued giving them the few coins we had.

One child we grew to like was Tess-foo. One Sunday evening as we were walking home from church, he followed us begging for money. That night we didn't have any with us, yet no matter how hard we tried to explain that to him, he simply would not go away. So I took him by the hand, led him back to our apartment where we fed him, gave him clean clothes, and sewed his old ones. Steven gave him his sandals and one of his toy cars. Before walking Tess-foo back where we found him, we gave him a *birr* (a bill worth about fifty cents). It was a lot of money for one so young, but we knew he would give it to his parents.

Every time we saw him after that his face lit up with a big smile. We were happy to see him playing in his new clothes, though it certainly didn't take long for them to begin looking like his old ones. His sandals disappeared within days —probably sold. Even though we didn't share the same language, we communicated beautifully in the language of God's love.

We fell into a routine: Steve and Larry flew every day, and Steven and I concentrated on his schoolwork. There were times of difficulty and stress because of Steve's flight schedule and my increased loneliness. My time with Steve was becoming more and more limited, and I was rarely able to share in the bush work. Steven and I lived fairly sheltered lives. Our apartment was completely surrounded by nationals who spoke not English but Amharic, a language that took a minimum of nine months of intensive study to learn. The Amharic alphabet alone has 233 symbols, which have to be learned before the structure of the language can be understood. The language was an extremely frustrating obstacle in our everyday life.

Because Steven and I had to walk everywhere, we really didn't get to know any of the other missionaries or foreigners who lived in other areas of the town. Steven had no children to play with, and I became his only source of entertainment, which left me little time for anything else. During his afternoon naps I caught up on Helimission bookkeeping records, did Bible studies, or played the piano. Our entire social life consisted of playing volleyball with the Baptists on Sunday afternoons and then again on Monday night with the people from the Society of International Missionaries. For all of us it was a good outlet from the stress of the work, and it gave Steven a chance to play with other missionary kids.

During our second month in Ethiopia, Steven and I were able to accompany Steve when he went north to some Southern Baptist feeding stations. It was wonderful to be back in a bush village again. As we walked through the village the children pressed around us in search of bread. The adults actually had to form a circle around Steven so he could walk.

Seeing our plight, some of the village men came out and threw stones at the children to chase them away. We were alarmed, but it intimidated the children and caused them to scatter for a while. But it didn't take them long to regroup and swarm around us again. It reminded me of the times Jesus was so pressed by the people that they almost crushed Him. As I watched little Steven almost being trampled, I could understand why Peter commented to Jesus about the pressing of the crowd.

The northern regions of Ethiopia are beautiful, and they have their very own Grand Canyons. Some of the landing zones were as high as ten thousand feet. The terrain was rugged and full of wildlife. We saw crocodiles, bush bucks, and large families of baboons.

The southern regions also have their claim to fame, for some of the largest crocodiles in the world live in the Omo River and the lakes of Arba Minch, a name meaning "Forty Springs." We also saw hippopotamuses in Arba Minch; in some areas herds of fifty to a hundred bathed in the muddy lake waters. The lakes also boasted the Nile perch, one of the world's largest fish and absolutely delicious no matter how they are prepared.

Eventually we were supposed to move to the southern village of Arba Minch, but we were waiting for special permissions for various needs and for a home. Our home was to be built from "sea-containers," also known as connex boxes. The boxes are smaller than a trailer, but when they are fixed up with windows, flooring, fixtures, and furnishings, they can be quite comfortable. Our home was to have a kitchen, an office, a small bedroom, and a bath. The master bedroom and living area would be built adjacent, with entry ways into all the containers. I thought it sounded wonderfully adventurous.

The famine tragedy of 1985, which was so highly publicized throughout the world, had given way to steady improvment, and the people were working hard to replant their fields. Yet when the rainy season came, little rain fell from the deep blue skies, and the realization sank in that the baby fields were still too weak to survive. Tragedy struck an even harder blow in July when swarms of locusts invaded the northern territories. In their wake they left total crop destruction and devastation. One swarm was so large it completely blocked the rays of the sun. Once again, the people of Ethiopia were left with little hope.

How would the world respond? News had filtered to the Western world that in the first famine food sent to Ethiopia was not actually delivered to the people who needed it because rebel activity had delayed every effort to dispense it. People in other nations were saying, "Why send money and food when it is only abandoned at the warehouses or destroyed? More than one million people died because the food wasn't getting to them."

Many of the rumors were true. There *were* efforts to stop the influx of food and medical care. The paperwork alone seemed too much for the young government to handle, and the fear it had of losing power was a real one. Still, we knew that although one million people had perished, another six million were spared, largely due to the efforts of relief suplies and personnel that had flooded in from all over the world. Jesus said, "I tell you the truth, whatever you did not do for one of the least of these, you did not do for me" (Matthew 25:45).

18
Questions

Being Christ's hand extended in a communist government was not always easy. Steve and I attended a church in Addis Ababa called the International Evangelical Church. All the Christian churches in Ethiopia had to be operated and pastored by foreigners. The national people were allowed to attend the services, but they were not allowed to preach, usher, sing special music, or teach. In spite of the restrictions, it was a rewarding experience to be able to worship with the Ethiopians. It was humbling to realize that the gospel was known to so many people speaking so many languages and dialects around the world. We serve such a big God.

One thing bothered me about the service, though. Every Sunday, the Scripture verse on the cover of the bulletin concerned the "full quiver of a righteous man." They must have had only a few covers to choose from because those Scriptures appeared constantly. It was as if God were forcing me to confront my fears about that issue. The passage I struggled with most was Psalm 128:1-4: "Blessings on all who reverence and trust the Lord—on all who obey him! Their reward shall be prosperity and happiness. Your wife shall be contented in your home. And look at all those children! There they sit around the dinner table as vigorous and healthy as young olive trees. That is God's reward to those who reverence and trust him" (TLB*).

Steve and I had the prosperity and the inner happiness that only come from Christ Jesus. As a wife, I was content in my home, in my husband's love, and of course, in the Lord's love and call on our lives. But I must admit that I had to take such passages before the Lord and wrestle with Him. When I looked around our table, I saw only one of three children. I was at peace about God's sovereignty, but I wasn't at peace about my feelings of guilt or about the assertion that children are God's reward to those "who reverence and trust him." Wasn't I reverencing and trusting God? Even more so, wasn't Steve?

Everyone had told me that the deaths of my children were not my fault and that God does not punish one of His children by striking down another, but I could not escape the passage in Hebrews that speaks of God's discipline and punishment: "My son, do not make light of the Lord's discipline, and do not lose heart when he rebukes you, because the Lord disciplines those he loves, and he punishes everyone he accepts as a son" (Hebrews 12:5b-6).

People were quick to say that those verses didn't apply to our circumstances. Our troubles may come about because Satan burns with desire for our souls, as he did for Job's and Peter's, and not because of any particular evil we have done. Yet, in spite of that truth and comfort, I did not want to miss anything the Lord might have been trying to teach me.

One Sunday afternoon after church I went to my room and put my thoughts on paper. What was Christ trying to bring about in me? To what was He calling me?

Dear Lord,

These are my thoughts on suffering as I believe you have shown me through Your word in Hebrews. Hebrews

* *The Living Bible*

168

5:8 says Jesus "learned obedience from what he suffered." Did He really need to learn it as we do? Or is it more an understanding of the obedience we need, so that, as the high priest who was tempted like us, He can know how to intercede for us to the Father?

Hebrews 2:10 says that He *was made* "perfect through suffering." Does this view suffering as a punishment for disobedience? How can that be when Jesus was perfect? How can He *be* perfect, and yet be *made* perfect? And His suffering was not for Himself, but, knowing our sinful nature, His suffering was a discipline He endured so that we might escape the "real punishment" of our nature. Jesus suffered for perfection, attained it, and was punished anyway for those who cannot attain it. (Ah! The Gospel!) So, if we suffer (or go through discipline), and it is not for the One who received our punishment, what do we suffer for? What is our discipline for? Should it not be to the same goal as the One made perfect already through this suffering? For, if we learn obedience through sufferings, then we receive joy . . . His joy . . . which is perfection. (How contrary to the world that seeks joy in this life only to find that it dies; yet our joy comes in death, death to self, and it is eternal and lives.)

What am I learning here? That Christina and Colby die, and that I do not understand; yet through their death, I suffer. I learn obedience to a deeper trust, to shed any guilt I carry for their death, and to believe more firmly in the hope that Jesus came to offer; and hope does not disappoint me. Colby and Christina are with Jesus. That hope is real. My suffering in their death is a discipline in understanding the eternal perspective of God's plan, not only for my life, but for God's testimony in my life to the world through the Gospel of Jesus Christ. I learn that God is faithful to His word, and His personal love for me reaches deep inside my heart as I am a vessel of His grace at work. He sustains me, He believes in me, and He gives me a desire and a purpose to go on.

If I suffer for perfection, then I know that God is disciplining me. If He disciplines me, it is because He seeks my perfection. Why? Oh, the wonder of this God! In all the

169

universe there can only be one reason: love. For, in my perfection to the gospel of Jesus Christ, I may dwell with Him face to face, assured of my position because of the cross, not ashamed, but completed by the perfecter of my faith. The cross of Jesus Christ's perfection through suffering, though it is mystery, is my way to become perfect as He is perfect for the fulfillment of my communion with the Father, which *He* desires.

Ah! To attain perfection! How deep a thought! To be perfect in every way! Yet God, in His wisdom, made a way to make the imperfect perfect. An eternal plan. Oh, what would man's plan be? Certainly not through hardship and sufferings. By works maybe. Outward signs. But do these change the inner man? How does one even understand perfection not ever being perfect? How would we know how to seek it?

The one who attained perfection, Jesus, must be our guide to perfection . . . and He is a willing guide. He does not assume perfection as something to be grasped, but as something to attain. He is the author of our salvation . . . salvation from sin . . . and salvation from sin is perfection.

"Your throne, O God, will last for ever and ever, and righteousness will be the scepter of your kingdom" (Hebrews 1:8).

How Great and Holy is the God we serve.

I love You,

Kathy

God was calling me to make a choice. It was easy to trust Him with Colby and Christina now. It was hard to trust that it was because of His love for me that He had allowed those things to occur in my life in order to shape my heart. It was hard for me to see how He answered my prayers to know and understand Him. I desired to love Him as He deserved. I wanted to love Him with a love that was real—not shallow or artificial or forced. I wanted to know how to really live free from the effects of sin by trusting in the work of Jesus Christ when He died on the cross for me. I wanted to be totally trans-

170

parent before my God, and I knew in my heart that God's glory would be revealed in my life.

> The unfolding of your words gives light;
>> it gives understanding to the simple.
> I open my mouth and pant,
>> longing for your commands.
> Turn to me and have mercy on me,
>> as you always do to those who love your name.
> Direct my footsteps according to your word;
>> let no sin rule over me.
>
>> (Psalm 119:130-33)

God was strengthening me and drawing me closer to His love. He was helping me to take my eyes completely off myself, completely off my circumstances, completely off man, and was directing me to walk completely in His power, in His love, and in His grace. Jesus Christ was indwelling my heart and becoming a part of me. "If your law had not been my delight, I would have perished in my affliction. I will never forget your precepts, for by them you have preserved my life. Save me, for I am yours" (Psalms 119:92-94).

Jesus says in Matthew that I am to take His yoke upon me, for His yoke is easy and His burden is light. When I looked to Jesus, trusted in Him, and believed in His eternal plan, my tendency to turn inward, to dwell on my pain, and to ask, *Why me?* began to dissolve. Instead, my vision increased so that I could see a bigger God and a bigger meaning for my life.

I remembered being under my parachute gazing at the world below me and wondering about how my life, which seemed destined to mediocrity, would fit into God's plan. Yet I was learning that Jesus desired to perfect and use my life so that I could share His redeeming love with a hurting world. My eyes began to open, and my heart began to understand just how deep His love for the world is. Although my suffering could never compare with His, it has enabled me to identify with the cost of sin for God and the cost of His great love for man.

I began to see how the pain of my growth could be "counted as pure joy" and to realize that God was expressing His love and perfection through me. Instead of asking, *Why me?* I was beginning to feel privileged to ask, *Why* not *me?* Why shouldn't I, a child of God, be used to give hope to a world that is dying in pain and tragedy? Why shouldn't I, someone saved from hell by God's grace, be willing to trust God for every area of my life? Why shouldn't I, living in a world filled with the horrific results of sin, be an example of God's love, promise, and peace no matter what Satan attempts to do to disprove it?

All those thoughts and questions penetrated my spirit as I considered what it cost to die to self as Jesus did. Jesus looked far past His own circumstances, kept His eyes on the Father, and trusted Him completely. Jesus always carried with Him the knowledge that His life, His purpose, and His death were not for Himself alone, but for the glory of the Father and the redemption of man. If I were going to completely identify with Christ, this concept would have to live daily in my heart: my life is not for me alone.

That evening I shared with Steve what I believed the Lord was showing me, and he sat quietly listening. I felt close to Steve as I sat next to him, and he comforted me and assured me of his love. As we talked of God's promises and God's peace, we were aware of the total strength of God's love uniting us in pain and in understanding. Many marriages would have ended in defeat when tested the way ours was, and surely Steve and I had shared many sorrows and joys in our marriage, but at that moment we had never been more thankful to God for giving us one another through it all.

19
Final Flight

During the next few weeks, our family had time to enjoy the activities surrounding our work. The International Women's Club in Addis had asked me to instruct their aerobics class three mornings a week, and since aerobics was something I enjoyed immensely and had taught in the past, I accepted. Three days a week a new friend, Carol Ann, picked up Steven and me, and we drove off to the Hilton Hotel. During the next two weeks Carol Ann introduced me to a number of the ladies who were part of the foreign community helping with the famine relief efforts. I finally believed that soon I would have some close friends.

Steve and I still played volleyball when he wasn't out in the bush. One Monday night on our way to a volleyball game Steve and I had what was for us a big disagreement. I had been taking care of the Helimission bookkeeping, and Steve was supposed to write down on a notepad the amount of money he took from petty cash each time he needed money. I then transcribed the amount into the ledger for permanent record. But keeping that record was not a priority for Steve. He had become quite lazy about it, and after he had not written down anything he spent for two weeks, I couldn't balance the books. So, on that particular Monday, I decided to *make* it a priority for him.

173

He assured me he would figure it all out the next day after his flight to one of the Southern Baptist feeding stations. The attitude expressed in the way he responded made me think he really didn't care—as if he were saying that he would get around to it if he could find the time. That made me angry, so I pushed harder, nagging him about the importance of accurate bookkeeping. He became sarcastic, and in return I became furious. Within minutes we were so mad at each other that we couldn't even talk.

We made it through the volleyball game on opposite teams, managing to keep our problem to ourselves, but our stubbornness stayed with us long after we got home. By the time we went to bed, Steve did make a comment about working on the receipts the next afternoon, but the argument was by then so pointless we both knew we were wrong. Too hurt, stubborn, and tired to resolve it, we let the sun go down on our anger.

The following morning, Steve woke up early and quietly got ready for his flight. He had his devotional time with the Lord and then unhurriedly shaved and dressed. Before he left, he came in and softly kissed me on the cheek. The kiss was softer than usual because none of his moustache touched my skin, and it meant a lot to me because I knew it said that our spat the night before was not a factor in our love for one another. I could go through the day without the weight of yesterday's argument hanging over my head.

A little later Steven woke up, came into my room, and pulled me out of bed so that I would make him some breakfast. The day was starting out as usual. After breakfast I assigned Steven some schoolwork, and I sat down to write a newsletter to our supporters. My mood was light, and I wanted to fully convey how happy we were as we settled down in our new ministry in Ethiopia, in spite of the increased work load.

I began the newsletter with a favorite verse about joy: "The Lord your God is with you, he is mighty to save. He will take great delight in you, he will quiet you with his love, he will rejoice over you with singing" (Zephaniah 3:17). It had been a tremendous encouragement for us to know that in spite of our turmoil through the death of our Colby, my illness, our move, my loneliness, and the increased demand of the work, it was within His power to quiet us and lift us in love to the heights of His throne room. I envisioned God singing a song over us in His love, yet I knew that we should feel privileged to sing praises to Him.

While I was writing the newsletter I got a phone call from our new friend Wally Eshenaur. With much happiness and triumph in his voice, he told me that we had been approved for the Baptist house for which we had applied and that we could move in as soon as we were ready. I was so excited! I couldn't wait for Steve to come home so I could tell him. Wally then asked if he could be the one to tell Steve, since they had become such good friends in the past two months as they flew together. I said, "Oh, no problem! He's on a short administrative flight. He's due back between twelve o'clock and one. Call then—OK?" Wally assured me he would, and we hung up.

Steven and I celebrated the good news by making macaroni and cheese for lunch. We were expecting Daddy to come home at any time. But as the day wore on, Steve didn't arrive. I continued to write prayer letters and finally put Steven down for his afternoon nap. Wally called again, but I had to tell him that Steve hadn't come home yet. We still agreed that he would be the one to tell Steve about the house.

Steven woke up late from his nap around 5:00 P.M. and was still groggy when we heard the doorbell ring. When I answered the door, I was surprised to find five people standing there looking at me: a pilot named Jim Baker, his wife, Darlene, another couple, and a young man I had never seen before. Pleased to have some visitors, I cheerily said, "My, it's an invasion!" For a moment no one said a word. I felt confused, then all of a sudden I felt the lateness of the hour and asked, "What? Is it Steve?" Jim silently nodded his head.

Panic ran through my heart. I knew immediately that he wasn't hurt. If he were, Jim would have told me something —anything. Yet he didn't go on, so I had to ask, "Is he dead?" Jim slowly nodded his head yes.

I let out a scream and sank to the floor. I cried and cried, asking God with inexorable grief, "No, God! No! Why? What more do You want from me? How much more do I have to give You to show You, to prove to You that I will go wherever You want me to go, and do whatever You want me to do? Didn't I just let go of Colby? Are you going to take Steven, too? O God, O God, O God—how do I stop this hurt? Even in Your will what will make this pain go away? O, my precious Steve—and now, he too, is with You. How should I tell Steven? How do I tell my family? How will I tell his father?"

I don't know how long I sat there and cried out my anguish to God, but those five dear people just waited patiently until I was finished. I knew I needed to call my family and friends back in the States. I couldn't imagine how they would take the news, but I knew I had to talk to someone who knew me, who understood my heart and my walk with God. I felt as if I were in a dream, but I firmly believe that I was able to go about the task of telling everyone, and responding in faith, because the Word of God had long before taken root in my heart.

The first person I talked to was my father. His reaction was the response I met in almost every person I spoke with: complete shock that this could happen so soon after Colby's death. I remember trying to express the pain that kept stabbing my heart. I hurt so much. I knew my father wanted to say something, anything, to comfort me. But what could he say? Beyond his effort to comfort there was only silence.

I felt so isolated. Here I was, newly arrived in a Third World communist country with only several acquaintances. Larry, the other pilot, had left a week earlier to go back to Canada on furlough, and there was no one in Ethiopia who really knew or understood me, what was in my heart, or why I was there. Why had God allowed this? How could He have permitted this after everything else Steven and I had been through?

It took me days to realize it, but I firmly believe that God let me receive this news when I was isolated so that He, and He alone, would receive the full glory for my healing. I marvel at the splendor of it. The healing of my heart was not going to come from man. It was not going to come from the church, or from my family, or from my friends, though they would be sources of great strength and encouragement to me. The actual transformation of my heart would be totally God's handiwork for His glory—so complete and so sure that there would be no question of His personal love and sustaining power in my life.

There was never any question as to the cause of Steve's death. I knew he had died in the helicopter even before Jim told me what he knew of the accident. Although at the time we did not know specifically why, apparently the engine had failed. Both Steve and his passenger, Troy Waldron, a Southern Baptist missionary, were killed instantly on impact.

After I had made a few phone calls, I went to see Troy's wife, Jewell, who was also just finding out about the tragedy. Only two days before, at a Sunday volleyball game, Jewell had told me they'd just found out that she was pregnant with their third child.

On the way to Jewell's house we had to drive down a dirt road past a military hospital. Across the street from the hospital was a soccer field, and it looked as though a game had just ended, for a crowd of patients was making its way to the hospital grounds. Every single patient in the mass of people crossing the street was either on crutches or bandaged heavily somewhere on his body. Our car slowed to a crawl, and as the crippled men separated on either side of the road to let us pass, I looked closer at their faces. Suddenly I was thankful to God that Steve was not alive to suffer as those men were. The emptiness in their eyes reflected deep pain.

When Jim, Darlene, and I arrived at Jewell's house, we found that many people had come already to show their love and to lend comfort. Although I recognized everyone there, it was difficult for me to feel a part of the friendships that had already been established among them. I knew that they too felt a bit inadequate in expressing their feelings toward me. Yet I was comforted by their presence and by the knowledge that they wanted me to be surrounded by their love as an extension of Christ's love.

That evening about nine o'clock Jewell and I decided to go to the hospital to see Steve and Troy. My feelings were extremely mixed, but I felt compelled to go. A group of us crowded into a mission van and drove a very long way through parts of Addis I hadn't yet been to. We came to a hospital that looked like a prison or concentration camp building. It was very dark, and spotlights were shining on the weather-beaten walls and entrances. We were directed to a back gate, and the guard allowed us to go through, once he understood why we were there. It was cold, muddy, and drizzling, but Jewell and I got out of the van and waited for Pastor Fahnestock, who went to inquire about Steve and Troy.

A short moment later he came out of the doorway that led to the morgue. There was only one small light bulb over the door, but in its glow I could see from his face that he was concerned. He talked briefly with another man, then walked over to us and suggested that we remember Steve and Troy as they were when they were alive. They had been badly injured in the accident, and it would be better if we didn't see them. He also told us that they were still in rigor mortis and that Steve had remained in flight position—one hand out front for the cyclet and one hand to his side for the collective lever.

"God love him," I uttered, "that was his favorite position." I knew that if Steve could have chosen how to die, he would have wanted to do it in service to Jesus in the pilot seat of his helicopter. We gathered in a small circle and said a prayer before getting back into the van with heavy hearts as we pondered the ways of God.

That night I stayed in a vacant apartment in the same building as Jim and Darlene. Steven had been taken there already. I had told him earlier that his Daddy died in a helicopter accident and had gone to be with Jesus, Colby, and Christina. As I was getting ready for bed, he came to me. With his child's faith and a smile he said, "Well, Mom, I guess this makes you a widow. You'll have to find me a new daddy now!"

I was shocked and couldn't help but laugh as I asked him, "Where did you hear that?"

He replied, "We just learned about Elijah and the widow in Sunday school this week."

That had been two days ago. My heart filled with joy as I thought of God in all His love teaching Steven the concept of widowhood only days before the accident so that he wouldn't forget it or be afraid of it.

20
An End and a Beginning

I slept badly that night. I felt uncomfortable in the strange apartment and kept the light on. Finally, around 3:00 A.M., I dozed off. At 6:00 I awoke and went immediately to my Bible. During my devotions, the Lord once again began the healing process of my heart, and He confirmed to me that my healing would come from Him alone.

> Find rest, O my soul, in God alone;
>   my hope comes from him.
> He alone is my rock and my salvation;
>   he is my fortress, I will not be shaken.
> My salvation and my honor depend on God;
>   he is my mighty rock, my refuge.
> Trust in him at all times, O people;
>   pour out your hearts to him,
>   for God is our refuge.
>   (Psalm 62:5-8)

We accept as common knowledge that God can save a sinner, yet we do not wholeheartedly believe that God can and will sustain a believer. Now, through the psalm, God's sustaining power began to work in me. The words gave me my first glimpse of personal peace in dealing with Steve's death.

God's Word—the Word He gave us to use—is filled with power, love, and insight into His ways that will help us in our personal walk with Him. His Word struck my heart deeply. God alone would be faithful to complete His Word in me. He alone would quiet me in His love. He alone would be my salvation, my rock, my rest, my refuge. I could depend on Him alone to carry the weight my heart bore, and I sensed His grace already surrounding me.

I went back to my own apartment, and as the day wore on many people came to visit. I received countless calls from the States, and there was a constant flow of love holding me as I absorbed the reality of Steve's death. It was a day to share and remember the beautiful qualities of my husband. I remember talking to Pastor Fahnestock, who had been just getting to know us as a part of his congregation. I wanted somehow for him to understand the sweet spirit that Steve had possessed, and I remember telling him, "Steve was naturally a generous person. He was the most serving man I knew; he would have made a great wife." With the last statement, I saw understanding dawn in Pastor Fahnestock's eyes.

The next morning was Thursday. We received word that Steve and Troy had been prepared for burial. The doctor said that if Jewell and I wanted to, we could see them. We had to go that morning because the funeral was scheduled for the afternoon. After picking up Jewell and a few other ladies, we drove to the hospital morgue to say our good-byes. As I stood on the porch before walking into the room where my husband lay, a feeling of overwhelming heaviness came over me. Words cannot express it. But God's grace enveloped me and gave me the boldness I needed to walk into that room. When I had said good-bye to Colby and Christina, it was a healing process that had helped me to let go. Now I had to trust God that I would experience some of that healing when I saw Steve.

The two coffins were side by side on the floor of a dimly lit, cluttered, dirty room. Steve's injuries were quite evident, and as I fixed his tie, all I could do was cry and say a small prayer of sacrifice to the Lord. Steve had been my best friend, and now I couldn't talk to him. I couldn't tell him how I was feeling. I couldn't share the pain of loneliness that was filling every part of me. Neither joy nor overwhelming praise to the Lord was flowing through my heart as I knelt there beside my husband. I only knew that my heart ached—ached deeply—and I could not possibly bear one more ounce of sorrow.

Before leaving the room, I went over to see Troy, a man I had barely known but significant now because he had been chosen to meet the Lord alongside my husband. From that day on, his memory became very special to my heart. I offered a prayer, and though my whole being ached to stay just one minute more, I left the room. I desperately needed to hug somebody. A doctor friend was standing on the porch, and he graciously gave me his shoulder for comfort.

I returned to my apartment alone to prepare for the funeral. My worker, Selamauweet, was there, but she spoke no English, so I knew I would have time to reflect and sort out my feelings before the service that afternoon. Slowly, I began to go through Steve's things and pack them. He didn't have very much. What little he did have was mostly clothes. I would be moving from Ethiopia in about a week, so it was a precious time to go through his things by myself at my own pace. Selamauweet stayed next to me in silence. I felt her love and compassion, and tears rolled down her cheeks as we silently motioned to each other and packed.

When I was finished, I went over to the piano. A song I had just written, "All My Heart," was on the piano's music stand. As I stared at the title of the song and slowly began to sing the words to the Lord, a flood of tears poured down my face. It seemed so difficult to give Him all my heart. Every time I thought I had given it all to Him, there was more to give. Yet that is what our walk with Him is all about: precept by precept, step by step. We are being molded and shaped into the image of Christ, are learning how to totally trust Him with our lives. I was so thankful for that time alone with Him to cry and release the tears welling up inside me, for even in my weakness, He was strengthening me and preparing my heart for the service that afternoon—the burial of another loved one. The thought of watching yet another coffin being dropped into the ground kept pressing on my mind, the image engulfing me, and my whole heart looked to the Lord. I knew that only in His strength could I go through the service.

Jim and Darlene picked me up at about 1:30. Steven was with Wally and his wife, Tannie. They would bring him to the service separately. The foreigners' cemetery was on the outskirts of northern Addis. It was a rainy, wet afternoon, and outside the cemetery gates we were delayed by a large traffic jam from another funeral. Nevertheless, we arrived in time for the scheduled service. More than four hundred people came to the ceremony—many of them Ethiopian officials and representatives from different government ministries. United States embassy personnel were there, along with representatives of many of the international relief organizations.

The cemetery grounds were rough, unkempt, and especially muddy due to the rain. Everyone came with their umbrellas and gathered around the burial site to wait. The mood was quiet and respectful but not gloomy.

Steve and Troy were to be buried next to one another, and Jewell and I waited with resigned acceptance for the caskets to arrive. The Ethiopian custom is to wail and moan loudly until the casket reaches a resting place beside the grave, and a part of me wanted to do the same, but instead I listened quietly to Tannie as she explained to Steven what was happening.

As the service progressed, the clouds began to break and the sun generously peeked through. By the end of the service umbrellas were down, coats had been removed, and it felt like the blue sky and bright sunshine had surrounded us with a warm heavenly blanket. God in His unending, deeply compassionate, intimately personal love embraced me with the image of His victory over death. Jim Baker said to me later, "It reminded me of the mourning of death breaking forth into a celebration of glorious resurrection!"

How true that statement was. I reflected on the death of Jesus and the darkness that overshadowed the crucifixion day. Jesus not only took the punishment for our sins but was separated from the love of His Father. The Father's anger poured out upon His only Son. Then came victory, and the glory of that Easter Sunday shone with all His resurrection power. I felt God speaking to me in a mighty way. He was indeed revealing to me how in my heartache I was "sharing in the fellowship of His sufferings." This fellowship was not just something I read about in a book, but a truth I was experiencing in my spirit.

More important, I was beginning to understand what "the power of His resurrection" meant. It is the power of His love to hold my heart and keep me from falling, no matter what the circumstances around me; it is His sovereignty in a world where the prince of darkness rules with a vengeance; it is His grace to save me from the power of that prince and the all-encompassing sin of my own nature; and it is His ultimate sacrifice to allow His Son's death to free us from the curse that not only brings about our physical death, but even more devastatingly, our spiritual death. Once again, if I had chosen not to trust Christ, the hope of my spirit would have been crushed under the foot of the prince who only comes to "steal," "kill," and "destroy." "For our struggle is not against flesh and blood, but against the rulers, against the authorities, against the powers of this dark world and against the spiritual force of evil in the heavenly realms" (Ephesians 6:12).

Christians are not exempt from the sorrows of life. If God had chosen to heal Christina, He could have done that easily. If God had chosen to spare Colby from the effects of the poison, He could have done so. If it were His will, God could have placed a hedge around Steve's life so that nothing could have touched that helicopter. Yet if we believe in God only for the blessings He can give us, our belief in Him is not based on love and trust but on our own selfish desires and our concept of what we think God owes us simply because we believe in Him. God desires that our love for Him be pure and holy, just as His love for us is pure and holy. We must come to the point where we can say, with Job, "Though he slay me, yet will I hope in him" (Job 13:15).

Some people confuse Christ's sufferings with a ticket to a life of pain-free ease and getting what they pray for because they have sought it "in Jesus' name." People have actually come to me and said that since Christ died on the cross and suffered for our sin we no longer have to endure suffering or hardship of any kind in this world. And since I obviously have have suffered, there surely must be something wrong with my walk with the Lord. These persons argue from verses such as Isaiah 53:5, "By his wounds we are healed," saying that the verse means we no longer have to suffer illness and disease because Christ was beaten for us. Not only is their interpretation in direct conflict with Scripture, but it fails to take into account that without the testing of our faith we greatly limit our understanding of God, His love for us, and the depth of Christ's sacrifice on the cross for our sin. How much better for them to have the apostle Paul's attitude concerning suffering: "Therefore, I will boast all the more gladly about my weaknesses, so that Christ's power may rest on me. That is why, for Christ's sake, I delight in weaknesses, in insults, in hardships, in persecutions, in difficulties. For when I am weak, then I am strong" (2 Corinthians 12:9b-10).

Death, illness, heartache, tragedy, loneliness, sin, greed, persecution, danger—none of those earthly things is the battleground. The battleground is the soul. Without Christ, we battle alone—and lose. With Christ, nothing in all creation can separate us from the love of God: "No, in all these things we are more than conquerors through him who loved us. For I am convinced that neither death nor life, neither angels nor demons, neither the present nor the future, nor any powers, neither height nor depth, nor anything else in all creation, will be able to separate us from the love of God that is in Christ Jesus our Lord" (Romans 8:37-39).

The key was to be in Christ Jesus. That truth was made even more real to me later that day as I drove our van through the busy streets of Addis Ababa. The realization that Steve was never coming back to me suddenly hit my entire being with unbelievable force. Sheer panic and and uncontrollable fear raced through my body such as I had never experienced before. It was as if God was letting me see what it would be like to go through not only this experience, but my whole life, without Him. He was allowing me to glimpse what eternity without Christ was like: total desolation. Separation from peace. Separation from love. And the presence of hell. In less than a second it was over, and I felt God's strength and grace pouring through me like rushing water, cleansing me of those emotions. God's personal love was again brought to the "dividing of the soul and spirit" within my heart.

The following morning, Friday, August 7, three days after the crash, Ernie Tanner arrived from Switzerland. I was so happy to see him and to feel that bond of belonging to someone. The other missionaries had been incredible in showing their love for me, but seeing Ernie made me realize again how lonely I felt inside. The compassion and sorrow in his eyes burned into my heart, and I drew strength from his understanding and love as we hugged and then began to talk about the accident. Lil' Steven was at a friend's house, so Ernie and I decided to go up to the crash site together. He never once questioned my need to go or insisted I stay home, although many other people had not understood my need to go to the site and had asked, "What could possibly be there that you need to see?" But as a pilot's wife and understanding aviation as I did, there were questions in my heart I wanted answered. I had to know for myself what had happened, what had been on his mind, what he had been trying to do in those last minutes of his life.

Within the hour we took off in a helicopter from the International Airport of Addis Ababa and headed north over the mountains. In ten minutes we were over the crash site. We circled the area so that Ernie could get a better understanding of the overall scene, but my eyes were captivated by the destruction below me. The helicopter was completely crushed, and debris was everywhere. The pilot directed our craft to a landing zone on a hill just above the wreckage. As I climbed out, my feelings escaped to a place far past my understanding. Many people were at the site already, going over the wreckage and trying to figure out what exactly had gone wrong. In addition to Ethiopian civil aviation officials, there were two mechanical engineers, George and Bill, whom I recognized from seeing them in the hangar in Addis. I made my way down the hill and asked them to tell me what they knew about the accident.

Bill said that Steve and Troy had taken off from Addis Ababa at about 7:45 on the morning of August 4 to take Troy to a Baptist feeding station called Alem Ketema. Approximately ten minutes into the flight, Bill said, Steve experienced a severe power loss or engine failure over mountainous terrain and a ravine that sloped down into a creek. As he made his way down the side of the mountain, he drastically lost rpm and rotor blade rotation. Had he attempted to land on the near side of the ravine, his forward speed would have caused the helicopter to slide fatefully into the creek. Instead, it looked as though he had tried to reach the other side, but by then his rotor rpm was too low, his speed was still incredibly fast, and he had no power left to cushion his landing. By the time he crossed the creek, he was so close to the ground the tail section hit a tree and broke off. The bottom of the fuselage struck the bank of a gully leading down to the creek, and the helicopter flipped over, killing Steve and Troy instantly.

George added that some villagers had seen the crash from the mountaintop and immediately went to help. Once they arrived and turned the helicopter over to free Steve and Troy, they had to carry them about an hour's walk to the nearest road, where they met some military police. From there the bodies were taken back to Addis Ababa.

As I listened to George and Bill's professional assessment of the events that had taken place and realized that with only a few variables changed they would have made it, I knew without a doubt that God had purposed Steve and Troy to be at home with Him.

It was almost the noon hour, and soon we had to leave the crash site. Ernie and I decided that we would return later that afternoon so that he could bring the wreckage back to Addis and salvage some parts. In the meantime, we went to the Society of International Missionaries' guest house to get something to eat. But for the first time in my life I was physically unable to eat. Even though I was incredibly hungry, my body rejected food, and I soon gave up trying to force it.

About 1:30 P.M. we flew back to the crash site in a helicopter big enough to carry the large pieces of wreckage in a net hung from an external hook. Once we were at the site, the pilot and mechanic discovered that the cargo hook was faulty. They flew back to the city to get another helicopter, and Ernie and I stayed.

While Ernie fiddled with the wreckage, I sat down near the tree Steve had first hit on his approach. I sat there on the hillside looking at the tall green mountains, the rich blue sky, and the white billowing clouds. Listening to the sounds of the babbling creek and the African songbirds filling the air with their music, I could not imagine a more beautiful spot for Steve to meet the Lord. Why *wouldn't* the Lord have wanted Steve? He was the most serving man I knew. He consistently displayed the fruits of the Spirit, and to the best of my knowledge, his thought life was pure. I could not remember one malicious word he had ever said about anyone. He walked with God, had a personal relationship with Jesus, and did his best to please Him in every way. God could have changed the circumstances that led to Steve's death. He could have allowed an extra one hundred feet of altitude or fifty more feet of ground space, but God had a greater purpose in His eternal plan for Steve and Troy and the loved ones they left behind.

As I pondered those things, peace flooded my soul. I was sitting on the hillside where my husband met the Lord, and I sang to God. I was no longer singing songs of sacrifice but of praise. They were songs sung by a heart completely free to trust in God's eternal perspective.

The crash site was an end and a beginning. It was the place where I let go of my husband and willingly gave him to my Lord, and it was a place where life once again began to hold meaning. God was restoring my vision and renewing my purpose. Suffering being "granted" presents itself as a blessing, or more appropriately, an honor. I had come to realize when I contemplated Colby's and Christina's deaths and my illnesses that Christ understood that His suffering was not for Himself alone, but for the glory of the Father's will in the redemption of a fallen and rebellious race. Now God was telling me that my husband's pure walk and his death were likewise not for me alone but were for the furtherance of the gospel and the expression of Christ's love to a hurting world.

Just as Jesus looked past His pain and circumstances to God's greater plan, I too, must do the same. Though God was drawing me to Himself in a way that I could not fully understand and in a way that brought me deep pain, He was also increasing my vision for ministry to a world that lacked His love and therefore lacked hope. "I tell you the truth, unless a kernel of wheat falls to the ground and dies, it remains only a single seed. But if it dies, it produces many seeds" (John 12:24).

I sat on that hillside for more than an hour, singing and meditating on the ways of God before I heard the distant roar of the helicopter coming around the crest of the mountain. By that time I knew God's grace and love had penetrated my heart and that I was going to be all right. As I reflected on the scene around me, I thought of something David said in the Psalms: "I lift my eyes to the hills—where does my help come from? My help comes from the Lord, the Maker of heaven and earth" (Psalm 121:1-2).

Soon the wreckage was being flown back to the city, and to start our last trip out of the mountains, Ernie and I climbed aboard the helicopter. As we took off, we glanced down for one last look at the place that caused us so much grief and yet, for me, so much personal victory as I let go of my limited understanding and trusted God.

That evening Wally and Tannie invited us over for dinner. Lil' Steven had been there all day, and he loved the opportunity to play with Katie and Peter, who were just about his age. We sat down to a taco dinner, and I marveled at how the Lord continued to minister to Steven and at the simplicity of his childlike faith. Ruth, a mission nurse who joined us for dinner, told me of a conversation she had overheard between Peter and Steven earlier that afternoon. They were discussing who was the strongest person in the world.

Peter said, "I think He-man is the strongest."

Steven argued back, "No, Mighty Mouse is the strongest." The two boys were pondering that possibility when Steven suddenly concluded, "No, God is the strongest."

Peter exclaimed, "But you can't see God's muscles."

"Oh, yeah. Well—my daddy can!" Steven boasted in knowing triumph.

Within ten days of the crash, after temporarily closing down our mission station, Ernie, Steven, and I drove to the airport to leave Ethiopia. Once through customs we had about half an hour to wait before boarding our flight, and we chose some seats near the window so that Steven could see the airplanes. Our seats also allowed me to look directly across the tarmac to the area where our Helimission helicopter had been tied down each evening. I sat staring out the window at the empty landing zone, thinking about everything I was leaving behind. I had only been in Africa fifteen months, and it had cost me so much, yet my whole spirit cried out in love for the people, for their need for God, and for the simplicity of the culture. It was a tremendous privilege for my family to have been a part of Africa, and I longed to stay where my heart felt at home.

Sensing the turmoil behind my stillness, Ernie slipped his hand over mine, sighed heavily, and said, "It's hard, Kathy, isn't it? But God knows you, and the memories and heartaches you are leaving behind will give new birth to the future that God has purposed. Every new day is a day that we can trust Him for eternity." Turning away from the window I fought back tears as I smiled at Ernie and nodded my agreement. He squeezed my hand, and as I gazed back toward the window, I saw my life completely interwoven with God's.

A crackling sound popped over the intercom system announcing our flight, and we quickly gathered our belongings together. Taking Steven firmly by the hand, I walked through the terminal door toward the waiting airplane, and together we pressed on to a new life after death.

About the Author

Kathy Bartalsky previously served the Lord as a missionary in Africa for Helimission, a Switzerland-based organization that uses helicopters to bring food, medical supplies, and the gospel to needy, unreached people groups.

Kathy has since founded STRONG*heart* Ministries, an outreach dedicated to building up believers and offering hope to the hurting. She currently travels throughout the United States speaking in churches, women's conferences, and Bible seminars.

Kathy presently lives in Black Mountain, North Carolina, with her husband, Jim Gipe, and son, Steven.

For more information on STRONG*heart* Ministries, please write:

STRONG*heart* Ministries
P.O. Box 1100
Montreat, NC   28757

Moody Press, a ministry of the Moody Bible Institute, is designed for education, evangelization, and edification. If we may assist you in knowing more about Christ and the Christian life, please write us without obligation: Moody Press, c/o MLM, Chicago, Illinois 60610.